AGES 7 to 11

everyday French

Bon appétit !

IMPORTANT – Permitted use and warnings

Jan Lewandowski

Credits and acknowledgements

Minimum specification

PC or Mac with CD-ROM drive and 512 Mb RAM (recommended)
Windows 2000 or above/Mac OS X 10.4
Recommended minimum processor speed: 1.3 Ghz

Mixed Sources
Product group from well-managed forests and other controlled sources
www.fsc.org Cert no. TT-COC-002769
© 1996 Forest Stewardship Council

Acknowledgements

The publishers gratefully acknowledge permission to reproduce the following copyright material: **GeoBeats Inc** for the use of the film clip 'Berthillion Ice Cream' from www.geobeats.com © 2007, GeoBeats Inc (2007, www.geobeats.com). **INPES** for the poster '*En mangeant et en bougeant !*' © 2008, INPES (2008, www.inpes.sante.fr).

© Crown copyright material. Reproduced under the terms of the Click Use Licence.

Every effort has been made to trace copyright holders for the works reproduced in this book, and the publishers apologise for any inadvertent omissions.

Due to the nature of the web, we cannot guarantee the content or links of any website mentioned. We strongly recommend that teachers check websites before using them in the classroom.

Author
Jan Lewandowski

Commissioning Editor
Juliet Gladston

Development Editors
Kate Pedlar,
Niamh O'Carroll &
Fabia Lewis

Project Editor
Gina Thorsby

Editor
Tracy Kewley

Series Designers and Cover Artwork
Sonja Bagley &
Joy Monkhouse

Illustrations
Moreno Chiacchiera/Beehive Illustration, Joanna Kerr/ New Division Ltd & The Drawing Room

Designer
Sonja Bagley

CD-ROM design and development team
Joy Monkhouse,
Allison Parry, Andrea Lewis,
Anna Oliwa & Haremi

Designed using Adobe Indesign
Published by Scholastic Ltd
Book End
Range Road,
Witney
Oxfordshire OX29 0YD
www.scholastic.co.uk

Printed by Bell & Bain Ltd, Glasgow
Text © 2010, Jan Lewandowski
© 2010, Scholastic Ltd
1 2 3 4 5 6 7 8 9 0 0 1 2 3 4 5 6 7 8 9

British Library Cataloguing-in-Publication Data
A catalogue record for this book is available from the British Library.
ISBN 978-1407-10203-0

Contents

Resources on the CD-ROM

Unit 1
Interactive flashcard: *Les repas*
Interactive activity: *Quelle heure est-il ?*
Photocopiable: *Quelle heure est-il ?*

Unit 2
Interactive activity: *Je mets la table*
Photocopiable: *Un set de table*

Unit 3
Interactive activity: *Le petit déjeuner*
Photocopiable: *Le petit déjeuner*

Unit 4
Interactive flashcard: *Des légumes*
Interactive activity: *Au marché*
Photocopiable: *Euros*
Photocopiable: *Avec mon panier*
Song: *Avec mon panier*
Translation: *Avec mon panier*

Unit 5
Interactive flashcard: *Des fruits*
Interactive activity: *Un petit bonhomme*
Photocopiable: *Un petit bonhomme*
Translation: *Un petit bonhomme*
Image: *Vertumnus*

Unit 6
Interactive activity: *La nourriture*
Photocopiable: *Salade de couscous*
Translation: *Salade de couscous*
Poster: *Nutrition santé*

Unit 7
Interactive flashcard: *Les magasins 1*
Interactive flashcard: *Les magasins 2*
Interactive activity: *Allons aux magasins !*
Photocopiable: *Allons aux magasins !*

Unit 8
Interactive flashcard: *Des glaces 1*
Interactive flashcard: *Des glaces 2*
Interactive activity: *Quel parfum ?*
Photocopiable: *Le vendeur de glaces*
Song: *Le vendeur de glaces*
Translation: *Le vendeur de glaces*
Film: *Berthillon*

Unit 9
Interactive flashcard: *Les boissons*
Interactive flashcard: *Les casse-croûtes 1*
Interactive flashcard: *Les casse-croûtes 2*
Interactive activity: *Au café*
Photocopiable: *Recette de croque-monsieur*
Translation: *Recette de croque-monsieur*
Film: *Au café*
Film transcript: *Au café*

Unit 10
Interactive flashcard: *Des légumes*
Interactive flashcard: *Des fruits*
Interactive activity: *Le déjeuner à l'école*
Photocopiable: *Menu scolaire*

Unit 11
Interactive activity: *Où habites-tu ?*
Photocopiable: *La carte des régions*

Unit 12
Interactive flashcard: *Les fruits tropicaux*
Interactive activity: *Ici on parle français*
Interactive map: *Des pays francophones*
Photocopiable: *Mots cachés*

Introduction

Introduction

The activities in this book are intended to be practical and enjoyable while at the same time laying some sound foundations for language learning. Most of the units can be taught independently of the others, while others build on previous units.

On pages 8–9 there is a grid linking the units to the KS2 Framework for Languages indicating the relevant strand and, where appropriate, objective, and using the usual abbreviations:

> O = Oracy
> L = Literacy
> IU = Intercultural understanding
> LLS = Language learning strategies
> KAL = Knowledge about Language

Introducing new core vocabulary

- Always make sure the children are watching and listening. Get into a routine of saying *Regardez !* (Watch!) – make a spectacles shape with your fingers or point to your eyes; *Écoutez !* (Listen!) – gesture to your ear;
- Choose the simplest phrases to introduce first – especially if they are 'cognates' (look or sound like their English equivalents). This builds confidence!
- Only teach a few phrases at a time – so, to start with, try, for example *en autobus* then *en train* and *en bateau*. Play a couple of simple games (see below) then introduce the others.
- Point to/hold up the flashcard as you say the phrase.
- Use gestures to reinforce the meaning – arms stretched out sideways for *en avion* (by plane); hands making 'turning wheel' movements for *en train* (by train) etc.

Games for practising vocabulary

- **Répétez si c'est vrai** – Hold up a flashcard or object and say a word or phrase. The children repeat only if what the teacher says matches the picture or object she is holding.
- **Secret signal** – Sit the children in a horseshoe shape so that they can see each other. Display all the vocabulary items learned in a clear 'list' form. Choose one child to be the 'detective' who will go outside the room (accompanied by a TA perhaps). Choose another child to be the 'secret signaller'. Explain to the children that you are all going to chant the words/phrases, starting with the one at the beginning of the list. When the secret signaller makes the secret signal (for example rubbing the forehead or scratching an ear) you will all start chanting the next phrase in the list. The aim of the game is for the secret signaller to avoid detection and for the class to chant the phrases for as long as possible.

Introduction

- **Quick whizz** – Put picture cards in a pile with their pictures hidden from the class. Make a play of 'shuffling' the cards. Ask the children to say the word or phrase together when they can see what it is. Take the top one and quickly 'whizz' it, picture facing the children, but making it disappear again very quickly. Repeat as many times as you wish. Keep shuffling and emphasising that it's a game. From the teacher's point of view, this game is about getting the children to practise words and phrases; for the children it's about being the fastest and most observant.

- **Fly swat** – You need two plastic fly-swats and a set of flashcards fixed to a wall or board with sticky putty. The class is divided into two teams and children take turns to come forward. The teacher calls out a phrase/word. The first person to swat the correct flashcard wins a point for his/her team.

- **Salade de fruits** – The purpose of this game is to get children listening (and responding) to language. The children sit on the floor in a circle. Choose a limited number of vocabulary items. Give each child a word/phrase to remember, so that several children have the same phrase. When the teacher calls out one of the words or phrases the children with that phrase must stand up and change places. Now and then, call out *salade de fruits* and all must change places.

- **Hot/cold** – This game is excellent for whole-class practice of a 'hard to pronounce' word or phrase, such as *Qu'est-ce que tu as dans ta chambre ?* (What do you have in your bedroom). The seeker is sent out of the room, while the teacher or child hides the object or flashcard. As the seeker re-enters the room, the class begins to chant the word or phrase repeatedly and rhythmically, getting louder as they get closer, or softer as they move further away, until the object is found.

- **Morpion** (noughts and crosses) – On your class whiteboard, or using an interactive whiteboard, draw a 3 x 3 grid. Stick a word card in each of the squares so that the children can identify their chosen square. Divide the class into two teams – *les cercles* (o) *et les croix* (x). Tell the class: *choisissez une case* (choose a square). Teams take turns to choose a square and a member of the team must say the word on that flashcard to place their nought or cross on the board.

Introducing the written word

- Make reading cards for new words and phrases, so that you can introduce the written form of the new language you have taught in a planned and systematic way.

- When you show the children new word cards, always get them to read them aloud with you, insisting on correct pronunciation.

- Ask the children to tell you about 'surprises' in the spellings (eg. silent *s* or *t* at the ends of words).

- Encourage the children to look out for rhymes and patterns, pointing out which vowels make which sounds in French. (eg. the letter *i* in *petit, il, avril* making a sound like the English 'ee').

The gender of nouns

- You may find it helpful to add a system of colour-coding to the word and picture cards (say, red for feminine, blue for masculine) to help children remember which words are masculine and which words are feminine.

- Always introduce nouns with a definite/indefinite article (e.g. *le parc, un lion*) never the noun on its own. This will help children to remember the gender of the noun.

How to use the CD-ROM

Here are brief guidance notes for using the CD-ROM. For more detailed information, see **How to use** on the start-up screen, or **Help** on the relevant screen for information about a particular resource. The CD-ROM follows the structure of the book and contains:

- 12 on-screen interactive activities
- 12 on-screen interactive flashcards
- Audio songs
- Film clips
- Images and poster pages
- All of the photocopiable pages including the song lyrics and English translations

Getting started

To begin using the CD-ROM, simply place it in your CD- or DVD-ROM drive. Although the CD-ROM should auto run, if it fails to do so, navigate to the drive and double click on the red **Start** icon.

Start-up screen

The start-up screen is the first screen that appears. Here you can access: how to use the CD-ROM, terms and conditions, credits and registration links. If you agree to the terms and conditions, click **Start** to continue.

Main menu

The main menu provides links to all of the Units. Clicking on the relevant Unit icon will take you to the Unit screen where you can access all the Unit's resources. Clicking on **Resource finder** will take you to a search screen for all the resources, where you can search by key word or Unit for a specific resource.

Resource finder

The **Resource finder** lists all of the resources on the CD-ROM. You can:

- Select a Unit by choosing the appropriate title from the drop-down menu.
- Search for key words by typing them into the search box.
- Scroll up or down the list of resources to locate the required resource.
- Launch a resource by clicking once on its row on the screen.

Access the glossary of French words and English translations. (See more information below.)

Navigation

The resources all open in separate windows on top of the menu screen. To close a resource, click on the arrow in the top right-hand corner of the screen. To return to the menu screen you can either close or minimise a resource.

Closing a resource will not close the program. However, if you are in a menu screen, then clicking on the **x** in the top right-hand corner of the screen will close the program. To return to a previous menu screen, you need to click on the **Back** arrow button.

Glossary

All of the interactive activities and interactive flashcards link to a glossary. The glossary will open in a separate window. Simply click first on the desired headletter and then on the French word to reveal the English translation. You can also click on the audio buttons to hear the pronunciation of each French word.

Whiteboard tools

The CD-ROM comes with its own set of whiteboard tools for use on any whiteboard. These include:

- Pen tool
- Highlighter tool
- Eraser
- Sticky note.

Click on the **Tools** button on the right-hand side of the screen to access these tools.

Printing

Print the resources by clicking on the **Print** button. The photocopiable pages print as full A4 portrait pages, but please note if you have a landscape photocopiable page or poster you need to set the orientation to landscape in your print preferences. Printouts of the interactive activities will include what is on the screen. For a full A4 printout you need to set the orientation to landscape in your print preferences.

Framework links

Unit	Oracy	Literacy	Knowledge about language	IU	Language and learning strategies
1	3.1, 3.2, 3.3 4.1, 4.2, 4.4 5.1	3.1 4.3, 4.4 5.2	**Year 3:** Identify specific sounds, phonemes and words; imitate pronunciation of sounds; recognise question forms. **Year 4:** Recognise and apply simple agreements; use question forms. **Year 5:** Recognise patterns in simple sentences. **Year 6:** Recognise patterns in the foreign language; notice and match agreements.	3.3 4.2 5.1 6.1, 6.2	• Play games to aid memorisation. • Practise new language with a friend. • Read and memorise words.
2	3.1, 3.2 3.3, 3.4 4.1, 4.2 4.3, 4.4 5.1 6.1, 6.2	3.1, 3.2 4.1, 4.4 5.1	**Year 3:** Identify specific sounds, phonemes and words; imitate pronunciation of sounds; recognise question forms; recognise conventions of politeness. **Year 4:** Reinforce and extend recognition of word classes; use question forms. **Year 5:** Recognise patterns in simple sentences; manipulate language by changing an element in a sentence. **Year 6:** Notice and match agreements; use knowledge of words, text and structure to build spoken and written passages.	3.3 4.2 5.1	• Use actions and rhymes and play games to aid memorisation. • Practise new language with a friend. • Read and memorise words. • Plan and prepare for an activity.
3	3.3, 3.4 4.2, 4.4 5.1, 5.2 6.2	3.2, 3.3 4.1, 4.4 5.2, 5.3 6.3	**Year 3:** Identify specific sounds, phonemes and words; imitate pronunciation of sounds; recognise question forms; recognise conventions of politeness. **Year 4:** Recognise and apply simple agreements; use question forms. **Year 5:** Manipulate language by changing an element in a sentence; apply knowledge of rules. **Year 6:** Notice and match agreements; use knowledge of words, text and structure to build spoken and written passages.	3.3 4.2 5.1 6.1	• Play games to aid memorisation. • Practise new language with a friend. • Listen attentively. • Ask for repetition and clarification. • Apply grammatical knowledge to make sentences. • Look and listen for visual and aural clues.
4	3.1, 3.2 3.3, 3.4 4.1, 4.2, 4.4 5.1, 5.3 6.2	3.1, 3.2, 3.3 4.1, 4.2, 4.3 5.1 6.1	**Year 3:** Identify specific sounds, phonemes and words; imitate pronunciation of sounds; recognise question forms and negatives; recognise conventions of politeness. **Year 4:** Recognise and apply simple agreements; use question forms. **Year 5:** Manipulate language by changing an element in a sentence; understand and use negatives; recognise conventions of word order. **Year 6:** Notice and match agreements; use knowledge of words, text and structure to build spoken and written passages.	3.3 4.2 5.1 6.3	• Practise new language with a friend. • Look at the person speaking. • Write new words. • Ask for repetition and clarification. • Read and memorise words. • Use context and previous knowledge. • Apply grammatical knowledge. • Look and listen for visual and aural clues. • Use a dictionary.
5	3.1, 3.2 3.3, 3.4 4.1, 4.2, 4.3 5.2 6.2	3.1, 3.2, 3.3 4.1, 4.2 4.3, 4.4 5.1, 5.2, 5.3 6.4	**Year 3:** Identify specific sounds, phonemes and words; imitate pronunciation of sounds; recognise question forms; recognise spellings. **Year 4:** Recognise and apply simple agreements; use question forms. **Year 5:** Recognise patterns in simple sentences; manipulate language by changing an element in a sentence; apply knowledge of rules; develop accuracy in pronunciation. **Year 6:** Notice and match agreements; use knowledge of words, text and structure to build spoken and written passages.	5.1, 5.2	• Use rhymes/games to aid memorisation. • Write new words. • Ask for repetition and clarification. • Read and memorise words. • Sort words into categories. • Use a dictionary. • Apply grammatical knowledge. • Look and listen for visual and aural clues. • Evaluate work. • Compare the language with English.
6	3.2, 3.3 4.2, 4.3 5.3, 5.4 6.2	3.1, 3.3 4.1, 4.2, 4.4 5.2, 5.3 6.1, 6.4	**Year 3:** Imitate pronunciation of sounds; recognise how sounds are represented in written form; notice the spelling of familiar words. **Year 4:** Reinforce and extend recognition of word classes and understand their function. **Year 5:** Recognise patterns in simple sentences; manipulate language by changing an element in a sentence; recognise the typical conventions of word order. **Year 6:** Use knowledge of words, text and structure to build spoken and written passages; use knowledge of word and text conventions to build sentences and short texts.	3.2 5.2 6.2	• Use the context of what they see/read to determine some of the meaning. • Write new words. • Sort words into categories. • Apply grammatical knowledge to make sentences.

Unit	Oracy	Literacy	Knowledge about language	IU	Language and learning strategies
7	3.2, 3.3, 3.4, 4.1, 4.2, 4.4, 5.1, 5.4, 6.2, 6.3	3.1, 3.3, 4.4, 5.2, 5.3	**Year 3:** Identify specific sounds, phonemes and words; imitate pronunciation of sounds; recognise how sounds are represented in written form. **Year 4:** Recognise and apply simple agreements; apply phonic knowledge to support reading and writing. **Year 5:** Manipulate language by changing an element in a sentence; apply knowledge of rules when building sentences. **Year 6:** Recognise patterns in the foreign language; notice and match agreements; use knowledge of word and text conventions to build sentences.	3.3, 4.2, 5.1, 6.2	• Practise new language with a friend. • Write new words. • Compare the language with English. • Plan and prepare for a language activity. • Look for visual clues. • Use a dictionary.
8	3.1, 3.2, 3.3, 3.4, 4.1, 4.2, 4.4, 5.1, 5.2, 5.3, 6.1, 6.2	3.1, 3.2, 3.3, 4.1, 4.2, 4.4, 5.1, 5.2, 6.1, 6.4	**Year 3:** Identify specific sounds, phonemes and words; imitate pronunciation of sounds; recognise question forms and negatives; notice the spelling of familiar words. **Year 4:** Recognise and apply simple agreements. **Year 5:** Manipulate language by changing an element in a sentence; understand and use negatives; use knowledge of rules. **Year 6:** Notice and match agreements; use knowledge of words, text and structure to build spoken and written passages.	3.3, 4.2, 5.1, 6.2	• Look at the person speaking. • Use context and previous knowledge/integrate new language into previously learned language. • Write new words. • Ask for repetition and clarification. • Use context and previous knowledge. • Apply grammatical knowledge. • Look and listen for visual and aural clues. • Use a dictionary.
9	3.2, 3.3, 3.4, 4.2, 4.4, 5.1	3.1, 3.2, 3.3, 4.1, 4.2, 4.3, 5.1	**Year 3:** Identify specific sounds, phonemes and words; imitate pronunciation of sounds; recognise question forms and negatives; hear main word classes; notice the spelling of familiar words. **Year 4:** Reinforce and extend knowledge of word classes; recognise and apply simple agreements **Year 5:** Develop accuracy in pronunciation and intonation; notice different text types. **Year 6:** Notice and match agreements; use knowledge of word order and sentence structure to support the understanding of written texts.	3.3, 4.2, 5.2	• Look at the person speaking. • Use context and previous knowledge. • Integrate new language into previously learned language. • Write new words. • Ask for repetition and clarification. • Use context and previous knowledge. • Apply grammatical knowledge. • Look and listen for visual and aural clues. • Pronounce/read aloud unknown words.
10	3.2, 3.3, 3.4, 4.1, 4.4, 5.1, 5.2, 5.3, 6.2, 6.4	3.1, 3.2, 3.3, 4.3, 4.4, 5.2, 5.3	**Year 3:** Imitate pronunciation of sounds; recognise question forms and negatives. **Year 4:** Reinforce and extend recognition of word classes and understand their function; use question forms. **Year 5:** Recognise patterns in simple sentences; manipulate language by changing an element in a sentence; understand and use negatives; understand that words will not always have a direct equivalent in the language. **Year 6:** Recognise patterns in the foreign language; notice and match agreements.	3.3, 4.2, 5.2, 5.3, 6.2	• Use the context of what they see/read to determine some of the meaning. • Practise new language with a friend. • Compare the language with English. • Plan and prepare for a language activity. • Use a dictionary. • Look and listen for visual and aural clues.
11	3.2, 3.3, 3.4, 4.1, 4.2, 4.3, 4.4, 5.1, 5.3	3.1, 3.2, 3.3, 4.3, 4.4, 5.2, 5.3, 6.4	**Year 3:** Identify specific sounds, phonemes and words; imitate pronunciation of sounds. **Year 4:** Use question forms; apply phonic knowledge of the language to support reading and writing. **Year 5:** Manipulate language by changing an element of a sentence; recognise the typical conventions of word order in the foreign language; understand that words will not always have a direct equivalent in the language. **Year 6:** Recognise patterns in the foreign language; use knowledge of word order and sentence construction to support the understanding of the written text.	3.2, 3.3, 4.2, 5.2, 5.3, 6.2	• Write new words. • Plan and prepare for a language activity. • Read and memorise words. • Pronounce/read aloud unknown words. • Use a dictionary. • Look and listen for visual and aural clues.
12	3.2, 3.3, 3.4, 4.2, 4.3, 5.3	4.2, 4.3	**Year 3:** Identify specific sounds, phonemes and words; imitate pronunciation of sounds. **Year 4:** Apply phonic knowledge of the language to support reading and writing. **Year 5:** Recognise patterns in simple sentences.	3.2, 4.2, 4.4, 5.1, 5.2, 5.3	• Use context and previous knowledge to determine meaning and pronunciation. • Access information sources. • Look and listen for visual and aural clues. • Use a dictionary.

Unit 1: C'est l'heure de manger

Objective

To learn everyday French words for mealtimes; to learn to tell the time in French.

Introducing the vocabulary

- Using 'Interactive flashcard: *Les repas*' on the CD-ROM, introduce the words for the main meals. Explain to the children that in France lunch is between 12 and 2pm and dinner is around 8pm. Children often have a snack (*le goûter*) when they get home from school as dinner is served late. Ask the children if this varies from their daily routine.

Core activities

- If the children are not familiar with telling the time in French, begin by introducing hours of the clock using a large clock face. Set the time to, say, 3 o'clock and tell the children: *Il est trois heures*. Give a few more examples, then set the clock to a different hour and ask: *Quelle heure est-il ?* Do this a few times, allowing the children to respond.
- Allow the children to practise telling the time in French using 'Interactive activity: *Quelle heure est-il ?*' on the CD-ROM. Double click on the times to hear them spoken.
- Showing the times on the large clock face, introduce the key phrases for mealtimes, for example: *Le déjeuner est à midi*.
- Give the children a copy of photocopiable page 34 (*Quelle heure est-il ?*), scissors and a paper fastener. Ask them to cut out their clock faces carefully and to write their names on the line in the middle. They should then attach the hands of the clock, with help if necessary.
- Ask the children to set the hands of their clocks in response to your questions, for example: *A quelle heure est le petit déjeuner ?* to elicit the response *A sept heures/huit heures*. Ask individuals to say their answers. Some children may prefer to give approximate times for meals, using *vers* instead of *à*.

Extension activities

- Using the large clock face and the extension phrases, gradually introduce minutes past, then minutes to, the hour. As in English, children will experience more difficulty with minutes to the hour. If appropriate, explain that *moins* means minus. It is not expected that the children will grasp this quickly!
- The children can then make new clock faces using the bottom of photocopiable page 34 (*Quelle heure est-il ?*) folding the sheet across the middle. The sheet can be enlarged to A3 if preferred.
- Let the children use the clock faces to practise the new times in pairs, groups or as a whole-class team game.

Cross-curricular ideas

D&T: To make a moveable clock face.
Challenge the children to design and make their own clock with moveable hands.

PSHE/IU: To learn to respect the differences between people and different mealtime traditions.
Discuss some of the cultural differences for mealtimes at home and in France. In France, bread is available at every meal. Parts of a meal may be served separately but on the same plate and the plate may be wiped with bread in between courses (this is not considered impolite). Cheese, yoghurt or fromage frais is always part of a main meal and there is usually a green salad with dressing. Wine may be drunk by adults at lunch and dinner, but many people drink water; there may also be a small cup of black coffee for adults at the end of the meal.

Resources

Interactive flashcard:
Les repas

Interactive activity:
Quelle heure est-il ?

Photocopiable page 34:
Quelle heure est-il ?

Preparation

Ideally copy the photocopiable onto card. (Note: only the top half is required for the core activities; the bottom half can be omitted initially if preferred.)

A large clock face with moveable hands; scissors; paper fasteners.

Interactive whiteboard

Five-minute follow-ups

- Use the clock faces for display. The children can set the hands of the clock to the time and write a caption to go with the time, for example *Je mange le déjeuner à midi*.

- In the hall or playground, or as part of a PE lesson, play *Quelle heure est-il Monsieur le Loup ?* – What's the time Mr Wolf? One child stands at one end with his/her back to the rest of the class. In unison the class call out *Quelle heure est-il Monsieur le Loup ?* The 'wolf' replies, for example, *il est sept heures* and the children advance seven steps. This continues until the wolf judges the other children are near enough to catch. He or she then calls out *C'est l'heure de manger !* and chases after the others to catch the next 'wolf'.

Tips

As you switch from one activity to the next throughout the school day begin to ask the children what time it is in French.

Key words

Core:

un repas – a meal
le petit déjeuner – breakfast
le déjeuner – lunch
le goûter – afternoon snack for children
le dîner – dinner

Key phrases

Core:

Quelle heure est-il ? – What time is it?
Il est ... – It's...
... une heure – 1 o'clock
... deux heures – 2 o'clock
... trois heures – 3 o'clock
... quatre heures – 4 o'clock
... cinq heures – 5 o'clock
... six heures – 6 o'clock
... sept heures – 7 o'clock
... huit heures – 8 o'clock
... neuf heures – 9 o'clock
... dix heures – 10 o'clock
... onze heures – 11 o'clock
... midi – midday
... minuit – midnight
C'est l'heure de manger – It's time to eat
A quelle heure est le petit déjeuner ? – What time is breakfast?
Le petit déjeuner est à sept heures – Breakfast is at 7 o'clock
Le déjeuner est à midi – Lunch is at midday
Le dîner est vers huit heures – Dinner is around 8 o'clock

Extension:

Il est sept heures cinq – It's five past seven
Il est sept heures dix – It's ten past seven
Il est sept heures et quart – It's quarter past seven
Il est sept heures vingt – It's 20 past seven
Il est sept heures vingt-cinq – It's 25 past seven
Il est sept heures et demie – It's half past seven
Il est huit heures moins vingt-cinq – It's 25 to eight
Il est huit heures moins vingt – It's 20 to eight
Il est huit heures moins le quart – It's quarter to eight
Il est huit heures moins dix – It's ten to eight
Il est huit heures moins cinq – It's five to eight
Je mange/Je prends (le dîner à six heures) – I eat/I have (dinner at 6 o'clock)

Language points

- The pronunciation of some numbers will change when telling the time as the numbers precede a word beginning with *h* (*heures*) – draw the children's attention to this.

Unit 2: A table tout le monde !

Objective

To learn everyday French words and phrases for mealtimes.

Introducing the vocabulary

- Introduce the words for this unit by using the actual objects. For example, hold up a glass and say: *C'est un verre*. Ask the children to repeat what you say.
- Consolidate learning by showing an item and asking: *C'est un verre ou un bol ?* and so on.
- Hide an item behind your back and ask the children to guess what it is. Ask them: *Qu'est-ce que c'est ?* (What is it?)
- Once the children are familiar with the words challenge them to identify the items by sound. Ask the children to close their eyes (*Fermez les yeux*) then drop each item in turn onto a table. (Practise this beforehand to check that the items are unbreakable and that each one is identifiable by its distinct sound.) Remember to say *Ouvrez les yeux* between each one.
- Move on to *Passez-moi … s'il vous plaît/Passe-moi … s'il te plaît* – passing the item to you or to each other.

Vocabulary extension

- Carry out the sound activity but this time ask the children to write and show the new words using mini whiteboards or paper. They will need to have seen the words written down beforehand.

Core activities

- Give each child a copy of photocopiable page 35 (*Un set de table*) and ask them to label, colour and customise a place setting. The completed pages could be laminated for children to use at the dining table as their personal place mat. You could also back each one with the key words so that it also becomes a learning mat for future reference.
- When the children have completed their mats, take them into the school dining hall and role play mealtimes. Once in the dining hall, invite the children to come to the table (*A table !*) and tell them to enjoy their meal (*Bon appétit !*). They should then practise using the vocabulary learned in the lesson (*Passe-moi … , Voilà* and so on).

Extension activities

- Demonstrate how to set a table in French using the extension phrases provided. For example *Je mets la table* (I am setting the table); *Je mets l'assiette sur la table* (I am putting the plate on the table) and so on.
- Introduce the prepositions *à gauche*, *à droite* and so on. Ask the children where other items should be positioned, for example: *Où est le couteau ? Le couteau est à gauche*. Introduce *au milieu* (see Language points).
- Give the children an opportunity to practise setting a table themselves. Alternatively, the children can complete 'Interactive activity: *Je mets la table*' provided on the CD-ROM.

Cross-curricular ideas

RE: To learn a simple grace in French.
Learn the following *Bénédicité* – a simple grace: *Seigneur, bénissez-nous et aussi le repas que nous allons manger. Amen.*

PSHE/IU: To learn to respect the differences between people and different mealtime traditions.
Discuss with the children how knives and forks are not always used in other cultures, for example most people in East Asia eat with chopsticks and people in South Asia usually eat with their right hand. Ask the children for examples from their own experiences. Encourage the children to think about the lives of people living in other places and with different customs.

Resources

Interactive activity:
Je mets la table

Photocopiable page 35:
Un set de table

Preparation

Real (unbreakable) items for setting the table: knife, fork, spoon, plate, bowl, glass, tray, salt, pepper, vinaigrette/water in suitable sealed containers

Mini whiteboards or paper

Interactive whiteboard

Unit 2: A table tout le monde !

Tips

Use the *sets de table* for display. Fix paper/plastic plates, cups and cutlery to the display board and label appropriately with captions and speech bubbles.

Music: To learn to sing in a round.
Teach the children to sing *Bon Appétit*. Lyrics, which are sung to the tune of *Frère Jacques*, are below. This can be sung as a round – perhaps at the beginning of the role-play activity.

> *Bon appétit, bon appétit*
> *Les amis, les amis*
> *Vide ton assiette, vide ton assiette*
> *Mangez-bien, mangez-bien*

Five-minute follow-ups

- In pairs, ask the children to draw with their finger on their partner's back the shapes of some of the new words they have learned. They should swap over once the shape is correctly identified.
- Hold up a French word and ask the children to draw the object on mini whiteboards or paper.

Key words

Core:

un verre – a glass
un bol – a bowl
une cuillère – a spoon
un couteau – a knife
une fourchette – a fork
une assiette – a plate
un plateau – a tray
la sauce (vinaigrette) – vinaigrette
le sel – the salt
le poivre – the pepper
l'eau – water

Extension:

la table – the table
la nappe – the tablecloth
sur – on
dans – in
sous – under

Key phrases

Core:

C'est un/une ... – It's a...
Qu'est-ce que c'est ? – What is it?
Fermez les yeux – Close your eyes
Ouvrez les yeux – Open your eyes
Passe-moi ... – Pass me...
S'il te plaît – Please
Passe-moi le sel s'il te plaît – Pass me the salt please
Voilà – There you are
Merci – Thank you
A table ! – Come to the table!
Bon appétit – Enjoy your meal

Extension:

Je mets – I put
Je mets la table – I am setting the table
à droite – on the right
à gauche – on the left
au milieu (de) – in the middle (of)
Où est le couteau ? – Where is the knife?
Le couteau est à droite – The knife is on the right
Seigneur, bénissez-nous et aussi le repas que nous allons manger – Lord, bless us and the food that we are about to eat
Les amis – Friends
Mangez bien – Eat well
Vide ton assiette – Empty your plate

Language points

Passe-moi is the command form. To make it polite *s'il te plaît* must be added.

- The teacher will use *s'il vous plaît* if talking to the whole class. The children will use *Passez-moi ... s'il vous plaît* if talking to the teacher, which is the more formal form.
- Highlight the *le* in *le sel* and *le poivre*, meaning 'the'.

Note: *au milieu* will change to *au milieu de* when it means 'in the middle' of and will need to be adapted accordingly, for example *au milieu de la table, au milieu de l'assiette* and so on.

Unit 3: Je prends le petit déjeuner

Objectives

To learn everyday French words and phrases for breakfast foods and drinks; to be able to role play breakfast time in French.

Introducing the vocabulary

- Using props, demonstrate what might be found on a French breakfast table. Hold up each item and say the word in French. Ask the children to repeat what they have heard. Point to individual items and ask: *Qu'est-ce que c'est ?*
- Ask the children to cut out the breakfast items on photocopiable page 36 (*Le petit déjeuner*) for use later in the lesson. While they do this they could practise saying the new words in small groups.

Vocabulary extension

- Play Kim's game to reinforce the vocabulary. Tell the children to close their eyes and remove one of the props. Ask: *Qu'est-ce qui manque ?* (What's missing?)

Core activities

- Introduce the key phrases to the class. Ask individual children what they would prefer, using the props as visual aids: *Tu préfères du café ou du chocolat chaud ?*
- Initially they will respond with the item only but can be encouraged to use *je préfère …*
- To familiarise the children with the new words, and reinforce the learning of Unit 2, ask them to pass items to you: *Passe-moi du beurre s'il te plaît*. Remind the children of other vocabulary and phrases learned in Unit 2 (*voilà, bon appétit, merci*).
- Once the children are familiar with the phrases and breakfast items, they can role play eating breakfast in pairs or small groups, perhaps assuming the role of different family members. They should use their cut-outs from photocopiable page 36 and perhaps their completed *set de table* (photocopiable page 35) as props.
- Invite groups to perform their role plays to each other in the classroom, or as part of a French assembly or day.

Extension activities

- Introduce the following additional phrases: *je voudrais, je prends, je mange*.
- Explain some of the grammar behind the phrases you are teaching. Introduce the children to the extension phrases.
- Once they have improvised their role play, children could prepare a script for it, checking their spellings against photocopiable page 36 (this could be left on display on the interactive whiteboard).

Cross-curricular ideas

Maths/ICT: To learn how to use ICT to create a survey and bar chart or pie chart of results.
Help the children to design a survey about what the class eats for breakfast (see Extension key words and phrases). Ask: *Qu'est-ce que tu manges pour le petit déjeuner ?* Use ICT to present the data as a bar chart or pie chart.

Science/PSHE: To be able to differentiate between healthy and unhealthy foods.
Discuss what constitutes a healthy breakfast. Hold up various breakfast items and ask: *C'est bon pour la santé?* (You could extend the range of items to include healthy options such as fruit: see Unit 5 for vocabulary.)

PSHE/IU: To learn to respect the differences between people and different mealtime traditions.
Discuss mealtime traditions in different cultures, starting with the difference between French and English breakfasts. In France, coffee and hot chocolate are often served in a bowl, and croissants or bread are dipped into these; tea is served without milk, often with lemon; croissants and brioche are very rich, and so are not eaten every day; customs vary by family or by region (for example, cheese and ham are popular in the east of France).

Resources

Interactive activity: *Le petit déjeuner*

Photocopiable page 36: *Le petit déjeuner*

Photocopiable page 35: *Un set de table* (completed)

Preparation

Real-life or toy versions of breakfast foods such as: croissants, brioche, butter, orange juice, cup of coffee, baguette etc.

Interactive whiteboard

Unit 3: Je prends le petit déjeuner

Five-minute follow-ups

- Play line bingo using either a piece of paper or mini whiteboards. The children draw or write five or six food or drink items in a row. Call out the items in turn but the item can only be crossed out if it is at the end of the row. The winner is the child with only one item left; he or she shouts '*Loto !*'
- Play a version of 'My aunt went to market': the first child starts by saying, for example, *Pour le petit déjeuner il y a du pain*. Each child in the class then adds an item: *Pour le petit déjeuner il y a du pain et du beurre* and so on.
- Play 'Interactive activity: *Le petit déjeuner*' from the CD-ROM – as a whole-class or individual activity.

Tips

Collect empty food containers and re-label them in French to use as props.

Key words

Core:

le petit déjeuner – breakfast
du pain – bread
du beurre – butter
de la confiture – jam
du chocolat chaud – hot chocolate
du café – coffee
du jus d'orange – orange juice
une baguette – baguette/French loaf
une brioche – a brioche
un croissant – a croissant
une tasse – a cup
un verre – a glass
un bol – a bowl (for coffee/chocolate)

Extension:

des céréales (f) – cereal
un toast – toast
du pain grillé – toast
un œuf – egg
du bacon – bacon
des saucisses (f) – sausages
du lait – milk

Refer also to key words and phrases in Unit 2.

Key phrases

Core:

Qu'est-ce que c'est ? – What is it?
Qu'est-ce que tu préfères ? – Which do you prefer?
Un café ou un chocolat chaud ? – Coffee or hot chocolate?
Du pain ou un croissant ? – (Some) bread or a croissant?
Je préfère ... – I (would) prefer

Extension:

Qu'est-ce qui manque ? – What's missing?
Je voudrais ... – I would like ...
Je prends ... – I have (literally meaning 'I take', used for food and drink)
Je mange – I eat, I am eating
Qu'est-ce que tu manges pour le petit déjeuner ? – What do you eat for breakfast?
mauvais pour la santé – unhealthy
bon pour la santé – healthy
C'est bon pour la santé ? – Is it healthy?
Il y a – There is/are

Language points

- Note the use of *du* (masculine), *de la* (feminine), *de l'* (in front of a vowel or h), *des* (plural) meaning 'some'.
- *Un/une* is used for *croissant/brioche* because it is a single object. *Du* pain is appropriate as it is *some* of a loaf of bread, not the whole loaf.
- Simple verb expressions can be used as questions: *Tu préfères un croissant ou du pain ? Tu manges du pain ?*
- Verb endings change depending on the subject (*je mange*; *tu manges*).

Unit 4: Au marché

Resources

Interactive flashcard: *Des légumes*

Interactive activity: *Au marché*

Photocopiable page 37: *Euros*

Photocopiable page 38: *Avec mon panier*

Song: *Avec mon panier*

Translation: *Avec mon panier*

Preparation

Plastic or real vegetables

Weighing scales, toy cash register and paper bags (optional)

Envelopes

Interactive whiteboard

Objective

To learn the names for some vegetables and how to buy vegetables by weight and pay for them in euros.

Introducing the vocabulary

- Introduce the vegetables from the core words list using real or plastic vegetables. Use 'Interactive flashcard: *Des légumes*' on the CD-ROM to hear the names of the different vegetables in French. Explain that *un/une* is for one vegetable; *des* for 'some'.
- Discuss with the children that vegetables are often bought by quantity and weighed. If possible, use scales to weigh out a kilo and half a kilo of an item such as carrots. Introduce the phrase *C'est un kilo de carottes.*
- Ask the children to count in French how many carrots make a kilo. (Check that the children know the French for numbers from one to ten.)

Core activities

- Explain that French people often go to the market to buy fresh fruit and vegetables and that euros are used in France.
- Distribute photocopiable page 37 (*Euros*) for children to cut out their own euros (or provide ready-made and laminated ones). Store these in an envelope for future use.
- Using 'Interactive activity: *Au marché*', introduce the key phrases to enable the children to role play buying vegetables from a market stall. In this activity the children need to try and work out the correct order for the sentences in the following conversation (they should know some of the vocabulary from previous Units).

Bonjour madame.	*Je voudrais un kilo de pommes s'il vous plaît.*
C'est tout ?	*Oui. C'est combien ?*
Deux euros.	*Voilà.*
Merci. Au revoir.	

- Encourage the children to gradually build up their own dialogue in pairs. If possible, model this first with a teaching assistant. Have core vocabulary and phrases on display for the children to refer to. (See Unit 5 for the names of fruit in French.)
- Invite pairs of children to perform their role plays for the rest of the class using props and classroom equipment.

Extension activities

- Encourage the children to include some of the extension phrases in their dialogues: *Je voudrais aussi, Ça coûte, Je regrette, Je n'ai pas de …*
- Draw the children's attention to the use of negatives and explain how these are formed. (See Language points.)
- Ask the children to create badges for the *vendeur/client* for their performances. Explain that these have different endings depending on whether the person is male or female.
- Sing the 'Song: *Avec mon panier*' with the children. Explain that the first two lines of each verse can be translated as: 'With my basket, I go to the market/What do you have in your basket?' (See photocopiable page 38 for the lyrics. An English translation is available on the CD-ROM.)

Cross-curricular ideas

Art: To explore different materials to create items for a market stall.

Make props, such as different vegetables and crates for a market stall display, using papier-mâché, collage, modelling clay or recycled materials.

Maths: To be able to count, write prices and calculate totals.
Explain how to do a rough calculation to convert pounds and pence to euros: 1 euro = 86p. (Check the current exchange rate.) Set some simple conversions, in English. Use euros for mental maths starters, for example:
Un kilo de petits pois coûte deux euros, c'est combien pour deux kilos ?
Un kilo de champignons coûte quatre euros, c'est combien pour un demi-kilo?

Five-minute follow-ups

- Make shopping lists of vegetables with prices – using squared maths paper. (The children might be interested to hear that in France squared paper is often used for 'normal' writing, not just maths!)
- Encourage children to use dictionaries to find the names of other vegetables not listed. (Note: this can be time-consuming and they will need help with pronunciation.)

Key words

Core:

le marché – the market
des légumes (m) – (some) vegetables
des carottes (f) – (some) carrots
des petits pois (m) – (some) peas
des pommes de terre (f) – (some) potatoes
des haricots verts (m) – (some) green beans
des tomates (f) – (some) tomatoes
un chou (des choux) – a cabbage (cabbages)
un chou-fleur – a cauliflower
des oignons (m) – (some) onions
des champignons (m) – (some) mushrooms
un, deux, trois, quatre, cinq, six, sept, huit, neuf, dix – numbers one to ten

Extension:

le vendeur/la vendeuse (m/f) – the stallholder
le client/la cliente (m/f) – the customer

Language points

- The vegetables are listed in plurals – apart from larger items, such as *un chou*.
- Quantities are most frequently followed by *de* (of), for example: *un kilo de petits pois.*
- Some nouns have masculine and feminine versions in French, for example *le client/la cliente* ('e' is often added to make a word feminine).
- Negatives are formed by adding *ne* before the verb and *pas* afterwards: *Je ne sais pas.* Note that *n'* is used where the verb begins with a vowel, for example *Je n'ai pas de.*

Key phrases

Core:

C'est ... – This is...
un kilo de ... – 1kg of...
un demi-kilo de ... – ¹/₂kg of...
deux cents grammes de ... – 200g of...
Bonjour madame/monsieur – Hello madam/sir
Au revoir madame/monsieur – Goodbye madam/sir
Je voudrais – I would like
Voilà – There you are
... et aussi ... – ...and also...
C'est tout ? – Is that everything?
Avez-vous ... ? – Do you have...?
C'est combien ? – How much is that?
Deux euros s'il vous plaît – Two euros please
Je voudrais un kilo de pommes s'il vous plaît – I would like 1kg of apples please

Extension:

Je regrette, je n'ai pas de (tomates) – Sorry, I don't have any (tomatoes)
Non, je n'ai pas de (carottes) – No, I don't have any (carrots)
Ça coûte ... – It costs... (an alternative to *C'est*)
Avec mon panier – With my basket
Je vais au marché – I go/am going to market
Qu'est-ce que tu as (donc) dans ton panier ? – What do you have (then) in your basket?
Un kilo de petits pois coûte deux euros, c'est combien pour deux kilos ? – If 1kg of peas costs two euros, how much is it for 2kg?

Unit 5: Salade de fruits

Objectives

To learn the French words for some fruits, vegetables and parts of the body; to be able to write a poem using this vocabulary.

Introducing the vocabulary

- Introduce the core vocabulary using real or plastic fruits, or 'Interactive flashcard: *Des fruits*', in the same way as previous units. Tell the children: *Écoutez et répétez*. Show and name each fruit and ask the children to repeat what you say.
- Practise the vocabulary by asking *Qu'est-ce que c'est ?* or *C'est une pomme ou une poire ?* Remind the children of the verb *préférer* from Unit 3 by asking, for example, *Qu'est-ce que tu préfères, les pommes ou les poires ?*
- Create and distribute fruit cards. The children can play various well-known games, depending on their French knowledge, from snap to giving clues about the fruit on a card for their partner to guess (*c'est petit*, *c'est rouge* and so on).
- If children aren't already familiar with the core parts of the body, you will need to introduce these for the next activity. Introduce the vocabulary as above, then practise by playing *Jacques a dit* (Simon says): Introduce the command *Touchez* and then play the game saying, *Jacques a dit, 'Touchez la tête'*; *'Touchez la jambe'* and so on.

Core activities

- Using photocopiable page 39 (*Un petit bonhomme*) explain to the children that you are going to read them a short poem (*comptine*) about a strange little man made of fruit: *'Un petit bonhomme'* (translation of the poem is provided on the CD-ROM).
- Distribute photocopiable page 39 to the class. Talk about the words that are easy to guess, such as *orange* and *banane* (cognates), and false friends such as *raisin** and *prune** (see Language points).
- Read the poem to the children and ask them to draw the little man according to the instructions. Point to parts of the body at this stage to make the meaning clear. Re-read as necessary.
- Read the poem again – some of the more confident children may be willing to read aloud – then allow the children time to draw and colour a more finished picture in the space provided.

Extension activities

- Ask the children to create a female version of the poem: *'C'est une petite dame'* or *'C'est une petite bonne femme'*. To do this they will need to know to use *petite* rather then *petit* for feminine nouns and *elle* instead of *il* for 'she'. Encourage the children to use a dictionary to find more words for fruit. They could start with some of the Extension key words provided.
- Now the children have learned *je mange*, *tu manges* and *il/elle mange*, you might want to introduce the full way in which other parts of the verb are conjugated (*nous mangeons*, *vous mangez*, *ils/elles mangent*). Note that *nous mangeons* adds an *e* unlike regular *-er* verbs.

Cross-curricular ideas

Art: To be able to create an original piece of art based on a painting by Arcimboldo.
Show the class the painting *Vertumnus* by Arcimboldo on the CD-ROM and ask them to say what they can see. (Introduce/remind the children of the phrase: *Il y a …*) Depending on what you have already taught in French, the children could also describe the colours, and state whether or not they like it. Use this as a stimulus for children to create their own portrait composed of fruit and vegetables. Ask them to use a dictionary to find the French words for their vegetables. The finished artwork can then be discussed in French, or labelled as a display.

Interactive flashcard:
Des fruits

Interactive activity:
Un petit bonhomme

Photocopiable page 39:
Un petit bonhomme

Translation: *Un petit bonhomme*

Image: *Vertumnus*

Preparation

Labelled fruit cards – one set per pair of children

Real or plastic fruits (optional)

Mini whiteboards or paper

Interactive whiteboard

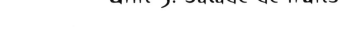

See http://wsgfl2.
westsussex.gov.uk/
aplaws/intergames/
play/Arcumboldo.swf

Tips

See **http://wsgfl2.
westsussex.gov.uk/
aplaws/intergames/
play/Arcumboldo.swf**
for an interactive
resource for creating
an illustration out of
vegetables.

D&T: To learn how to use levers and linkages to create a pop-up story book.
Make a pop-up story book of the poem using levers and linkages – each verse
of the poem could be a separate page with its own pop-up. The completed
books can be evaluated in French, using positive words (*C'est très bon/
coloré/original/drôle; Je préfère ce livre*).

Five-minute follow-ups

- Put plastic fruits in a feely bag: individual children have to put their hand in the bag and guess the fruit they are touching in French.
- Mime eating a fruit or vegetable: the children have to name what is being eaten in French.
- Children can practise the names of different fruits and parts of the body using 'Interactive activity: *Un petit bonhomme*'. Double click on the words to hear them spoken.

Key words

Core:

une pomme – an apple
une orange – an orange
une poire – a pear
une banane – a banana
des fruits (m) – (some) fruit
*un raisin** – a grape
la/sa tête – the/his head
le/son bras – the/his arm
les bras – the/his arms
le/son nez – the/his nose
le/son corps – the/his body
la/sa jambe – the/his leg
la/sa bouche – the/his mouth
les/ses oreilles – the/his ears
le/son pied – the/his foot
la/sa main – the/his hand

Extension:

un melon – a melon
un ananas – a pineapple
une cerise – a cherry
une framboise – a raspberry
*une prune** – a plum
un citron – a lemon
une pêche – a peach

Key phrases

Core:

Ecoutez et répétéz – listen and repeat
Je mange – I eat, I am eating
C'est ... – This is... /It is...
C'est petit – It is small
C'est rouge – It is red
un petit bonhomme – a little man
Touchez (le nez) – Touch (your nose)
Il y a ... – There is/there are...

Extension:

Il/elle mange – He/ she is eating
une petite bonne femme/une petite dame – a little lady
C'est très bon – It's very good
C'est très coloré – It's very colourful
C'est très original – It's very original
C'est très drôle – It's very funny
La présentation est très bonne – It's nicely presented
Je préfère ce livre – I prefer this book

Language points

- The children will be introduced to the possessive adjectives *son* (m), *sa* (f), *ses* (m/f pl). In the poem *Un petit bonhomme* all three words mean 'his'. If appropriate, you may wish to mention that *son, sa, ses* can also mean 'her'. (See Extension activities.)
- Many of the fruit words are cognates. This means that they are similar or the same as fruit words in English. The words with * are known as false friends (*les faux amis*). False friends are pairs of words in two languages that look and or sound similar but have different meanings (see also Unit 9). They should be brought to the children's attention.

Unit 6: Je mange bien, je mange sain

Objective

To know everyday French words and phrases for types of food.

Introducing the vocabulary

- Tell the children that they are going to learn more words for foods. Explain that the word for food in general is **la nourriture**. Ask: *Does it look a little like an English word?* (nourishment)

- Begin by asking what words the children already know. They should have many suggestions for fruits and vegetables from Units 4 and 5. They should also know some words for breakfast foods from Unit 3. As the children suggest words, make a list of them on the board, arranged under the following headings:

  > *les légumes et les fruits*
  > *la viande, le poisson et les œufs*
  > *les produits laitiers*
  > *les pommes de terre et les céréales*
  > *les produits sucrés et salés*

- Go through the core words list and write on the board any words that the children haven't already suggested, omitting **couscous** at this stage. Can the children guess what the words mean? For **les pâtes,** tell the children to apply the circumflex rule (add an 's') and ask if they can guess what it is (pasta).

Core activities

- Briefly talk to the children about the different food groups and ask what they know about eating healthily, for example: we shouldn't eat too many sugary and salty foods; we should eat at least five portions of fruit or vegetables every day. Revise the phrases *C'est bon/mauvais pour la santé* from Unit 3 by asking questions about specific foods.

- Tell the children that you are going to write a healthy recipe in French. Show them some uncooked couscous and ask if they can guess what it is. Explain that it is a popular food in France and comes originally from North Africa.

- Demonstrate in front of the class how to make the couscous salad, following the recipe on the photocopiable page (*Salade de couscous*) from the CD-ROM and explaining what to do in French. **Safety note: Care must be taken when using hot water in the classroom.**

- Make a list of the core phrases marked * (see Language points) on the whiteboard and ask the children to write the recipe using the writing frame below. Go through the writing frame first, checking that the children understand all of the verbs.

Prenez les ingrédients : ...	*1. Lavez ...*	*3. Coupez ...*	*5. Ajoutez ...*
	2. Prenez ...	*4. Mettez ...*	*6. Remuez ...*

Extension activities

- Show the children the 'Poster: *Nutrition santé*' from the CD-ROM. Explain that it was designed in the form of a hopscotch pattern to encourage French school children to eat healthily. French children also play hopscotch; they call it **la marelle**. Discuss with the children how to play hopscotch.

- Remind the children of the food groups and go through the poster from bottom to top, looking at the different foods. Do the children know the names of any of the foods in French? Explain that you do not expect them to know every word but they may be able to guess some of them from their knowledge of healthy eating. They could look up some of the other words in a French-English dictionary.

Resources

Interactive activity:
La nourriture

Photocopiable page:
Salade de couscous

Translation: *Salade de couscous*

Poster: *Nutrition santé*

Preparation

Plastic foods or pictures for the core words below (optional)

Ingredients to make couscous salad: couscous, sweet peppers, onions, raisins, tomatoes, sweetcorn, salt, pepper, herbs, vinaigrette; bowl, kettle to boil water, fork.

Interactive whiteboard

Unit 6: Je mange bien, je mange sain

Cross-curricular ideas

D&T: To make a healthy salad.
Challenge the children to design and make their own healthy salad recipe.
Drama: Invite the children to show the rest of the class how to make their salads in French, perhaps playing the part of a French TV chef.

Five-minute follow-ups

- Compare the *Nutrition santé* poster with the 'Eat-well plate' which can be downloaded from **www.eatwell.gov.uk/healthydiet/eatwellplate/** Is the UK nutritional advice the same or similar to France?
- Play 'Interactive activity: *La nourriture*' – as a whole-class or individual activity.

Key words

Core:
la nourriture – food
les céréales (f) – cereals
le pain – bread
le riz – rice
les pommes de terre (f) – potatoes
les pâtes (f) – pasta
le couscous – couscous
les fruits (m) *et les légumes* (m) – fruits and vegetables
les haricots (m) – beans
un poivron rouge/vert/jaune – a red/green/yellow pepper
un oignon – an onion

les raisins secs (m) – raisins
une tomate – a tomato
le maïs – sweetcorn
la viande – meat
le poisson – fish
les œufs (m) – eggs
les produits laitiers (m) – milk products
le lait – milk
le fromage – cheese
le yaourt – yoghurt
les produits sucrés et salés (m) – salty and sugary foods
les bonbons (m) – sweets
le chocolat – chocolate

les chips (m) – crisps
* *les légumes* (m) – the vegetables
Lavez ... – Wash...
Coupez ... – Cut...
Mettez ... – Put...
Ajoutez ... – Add...
Remuez ... – Mix...

Extension:
la marelle – hopscotch
surgelé – frozen
gras – fatty

(For lists of common vegetables and fruits see Units 4 and 5.)

Key Phrases

Core:
Prenez les ingrédients ... – Take the ingredients...
* *250 grammes de couscous préparé* – 250 grammes of prepared couscous
* *en petits morceaux* – into small pieces
* *tous les ingrédients* (m) – all the ingredients
* *dans un bol* – in a bowl
* *du sel* – some salt
* *du poivre* – some pepper
* *des fines herbes* (f) – some herbs

* *un peu de sauce vinaigrette* – a little vinaigrette

Extension:
une petite bôite – a small tin
la vinaigrette pré-preparée – ready-made vinaigrette sauce
Versez ... – Pour...
Laissez ... – Leave...
pendant dix minutes – for 10 minutes

une ou deux fois par jour – once or twice a day
au moins cinq par jour – at least five a day
à chaque repas selon l'appétit – at every meal according to appetite
à volonté – as much as you like
limiter la consommation – eat sparingly (limit the consumption)

Language points

- Categories of food start with *le, la, l', les* eg *j'aime les pâtes* – I like pasta.
- Colours follow the noun they describe eg *un poivron vert/rouge/jaune.*
- *Pâtes* (pasta) and *pâté* (pâté) are different; use these examples to show the children how an accent can affect the meaning and the pronunciation.

Unit 7: Allons aux magasins !

Objectives

To learn the names of the different French food shops and some words for packaging; to learn some strategies for 'decoding' new words; to know some similarities and differences between shops in their own locality and shops in France.

Introducing the vocabulary

- Give each child a copy of photocopiable page 40 (*Allons aux magasins !*) and ask them to cut out the word cards that are shown on the photocopied page.
- Explain that all of the words are types of French shops. (Most towns in France still have specialist independent food shops but, just as in the UK, people do a lot of their food shopping in supermarkets.) Tell the children that you are not going to tell them what the words mean but you will help them to say the words.
- Go through the pronunciation of each word in order, asking the children to repeat them a couple of times. You could use both 'Interactive flashcard: *Les magasins 1*' and 'Interactive flashcard: *Les magasins 2*' for this.
- Give the children a set time limit to try and work out what each word means. Explain that they are looking for clues about the meaning of the words.
- When the time limit is up go through their suggestions. (You could display and annotate a copy of the photocopiable page on the interactive whiteboard.) Ask the children which words they found easiest to work out. (Probably *le marché, le supermarché* and *l'hypermarché.*)
- Go through the children's suggestions and discuss how they arrived at their conclusions. Reveal the answer if they have guessed the correct meaning.
- Offer clues where they haven't guessed correctly: *la pâtisserie* – has a 'hat' over the 'a' (a circumflex) which tells you that once there used to be an 's' after the 'a'. Ask: Does it help to add an 's'? This should, with luck, elicit the word 'pastry'. Can the children work out *la confiserie* by looking at the first four or five letters? (confectionary)

Vocabulary extension

- Explain to the children that dictionaries can be really useful. Select children to find out the meaning of any unknown words in the dictionary. (Note: dictionary definitions of *la charcuterie* will vary from one dictionary to another!)

Core activities

- Look closely at the shops and ask the children if they know any French words for types of food they might expect to buy in each shop. (They should know some fruits, vegetables and breakfast items from previous units.)
- Challenge the children to use what they have just learned, along with dictionaries, to draw and label a typical French street, or a single shop in more detail.

Extension activities

- Set a role-play task where the children have to buy food for a picnic.
- Using the empty packaging introduce and practise the extension phrases.
- Referring to photocopiable page 40 (*Allons aux magasins !*), ask them which shops they would go to for the items they want. (See also vocabulary from Units 4 and 5).
- Before the children set off shopping, they need to make a shopping list. Use the phrase *Je vais aux magasins pour acheter ...* as a writing frame, substituting the different shops: *Je vais à la charcuterie pour acheter du pâté* and so on.

Resources

Interactive flashcards:
Les magasins 1
Les magasins 2

Interactive activity:
Allons aux magasins !

Photocopiable page 37:
Euros

Photocopiable page 40:
Allons aux magasins !

Preparation

Scissors, empty food boxes, packets, plastic bottles and so on (French, or English packaging relabelled with words from the extension phrases)

Euro coins created from photocopiable page 37: *Euros*

Interactive whiteboard

Unit 7: Allons aux magasins !

Tips

If you visit France, collect free supplements from hypermarkets to use for up-to-date price and product information and classroom displays.

Cross-curricular ideas

Maths: To practise counting, multiplying and estimating skills.

Extend the role play above by giving the children a set amount of euros each to buy their picnic. Invite them to work in groups and pool their euros to make their money go further. Ask the groups to make a shopping list of the items they want to buy. If possible, give the children some examples of prices and ask them to write the amount in euros against each item. They can then estimate how much they think they would need for their group's picnic.

PSHE: To plan a healthy picnic.

When the children have completed their shopping lists and role plays discuss the contents of their picnics and how healthy they are. Ask them to amend their lists to make them more healthy/balanced.

Geography: To know some differences between French and British shops.

Create a display that compares French shops (using photocopiable page 40) to a row of shops in Britain. Children could draw and label their own illustrations, or you could take photographs of shops in your local community.

Five-minute follow-ups

- Play the memory game *Je vais aux magasins pour acheter …* where each child adds an item to the list.
- Complete 'Interactive activity: *Allons aux magasins !*'

Key words

Core:

un magasin – a shop
la charcuterie – the cooked meat shop and delicatessen
la pâtisserie – the cake shop
la boulangerie – the bakery
l'épicerie (f) – the grocery
la poissonnerie – the fishmonger
la crémerie – the dairy shop
la fromagerie – the cheese shop
la boucherie – the butcher
le marché – the market
le supermarché – the supermarket
l'hypermarché – the hypermarket, superstore
la confiserie – the sweet shop

Extension:

un pique-nique – a picnic
une baguette – a French loaf
un gâteau – a cake
une quiche – a quiche
des fruits (m) – (some) fruit
des bonbons (m) – (some) sweets
du pâté – (some) pâté

Key phrases

Extension:

Je vais aux magasins pour acheter … – I am going to the shops to buy...
un paquet de biscuits – a packet of biscuits
un morceau de fromage – a piece of cheese
une tranche de jambon – a slice of ham
un pot de yaourt – a pot of yoghurt
une boîte de thon – a tin of tuna
une bouteille d'eau (minérale) – a bottle of (mineral) water

Language points

- All shops listed ending in '*erie*' are feminine.
- Quantities are always followed by *de* unless the next word begins with a vowel, for example *une bouteille d'eau*.
- Remind the children that if they want to buy more than one they will need to say or write the number and add an *s* when writing the packaging word, for example: *deux paquets de biscuits*.

Unit 8: Je voudrais une glace

Objective

To know everyday French words and phrases for buying ice creams.

Introducing the vocabulary

- Show the ice cream to the children and say *C'est une glace*. The children repeat this. Pretend to lick the ice cream. Say *Mmm, c'est délicieux. J'aime les glaces*. Ask individual children if they like ice cream: *Tu aimes les glaces ?*
- If you have completed Unit 4 remind the children of how they asked for vegetables. Ask: Can anyone explain how to ask for an ice cream? (*Je voudrais une glace s'il vous plaît.*) The children can practise saying this to their partner.
- Introduce the three core flavours (*vanille, chocolat, fraise*) using the different model ice creams. Ask the children to repeat each flavour, ensuring good pronunciation.
- Introduce and practise additional flavours using 'Interactive flashcard: *Des glaces 1*' and 'Interactive flashcard: *Des glaces 2*' .
- Use the 'Interactive activity: *Quel parfum ?*' to practise reading and pronouncing different flavours. Double click on the ice-cream flavours to hear them spoken.
- Give the children the opportunity to practise asking for the flavours as a class or in pairs: *Je voudrais une glace (au) chocolat s'il vous plaît* and so on. See notes in Language points.

Vocabulary extension

- Encourage the children to answer questions in full sentences: *J'adore les glaces* or *Je n'aime pas les glaces* rather than *Oui* or *Non*.
- Explain that the ice cream seller might ask what flavour you want: *Quel parfum ?* When replying to this a single word answer (plus *s'il vous plaît*) will be sufficient: *Fraise, s'il vous plaît*. The ice-cream seller might also ask how many scoops they would like: *Combien de boules ?*

Core activities

- Play 'Song: *Le vendeur de glaces*' from the CD-ROM. How many flavours of ice cream can the children identify?
- Share the lyrics using photocopiable page 41 and sing the song together. (A translation of the lyrics is provided on the CD-ROM.)
- Give the children time to role play ordering ice creams. Encourage them to use vocabulary they have learned in previous units: *voilà, merci, au revoir, c'est tout ? c'est combien ?* and so on. They could also use the euros created from photocopiable page 37.

Extension activities

- Once the children have practised their role-plays, they could attempt to write a playscript. An additional challenge would be to create a text in a different form, such as a poster advertising an ice-cream parlour. You may want to introduce possessives for this (*mes glaces sont délicieuses*). Dictionaries may also be required.
- Watch 'Film: *Berthillon*' to give the children an insight into what a French ice-cream parlour might look like. You could set some focus questions, for example:
  1. The lady in the shop, Murielle Delpuech, is the granddaughter of *Monsieur Berthillon*. Can you find the French word for granddaughter? (*La petite-fille*.) What does this literally mean? ('Little girl'.)
  2. Where exactly is the ice cream made? (Behind the shop.)
  3. What flavours do Japanese people prefer? (Fruit and exotic.)
  4. What do American people like in their ice creams? (Chunks.) Can you find the French word for this? (*Morceaux*.)

Resources

Interactive flashcards:
Des glaces 1
Des glaces 2

Interactive activity:
Quel parfum ?

Photocopiable page 41:
Le vendeur de glaces

Song: *Le vendeur de glaces*

Translation: *Le vendeur de glaces*

Film: *Berthillon*

Preparation

Ice creams made from card and coloured tissue paper (vanilla, strawberry and chocolate)

Euro coins created from photocopiable page 37: *Euros* (optional)

Interactive whiteboard

Unit 8: Je voudrais une glace

Tips

If organising a whole-school French Day, real ice creams, in the basic flavours, can be used and children can buy their own with the photocopied euros.

Cross-curricular ideas

D&T: To be able to make model ice creams for props/display.

The children could make their own ice-cream cones to use in their role plays: cut a semicircle out of card and role into a cone shape; add different coloured balls of tissue paper for the ice cream.

Music: To practise singing in unison and using untuned percussion.

Children can prepare a performance of the song in small groups, using percussion instruments to accompany their performance.

Five-minute follow-ups

- Play the well-known circle game Fruit Salad (*salade de fruits*) using ice-cream flavours .

Key words

Core:

une glace – an ice cream
vanille (f) – vanilla
fraise (f) – strawberry
chocolat (m) – chocolate
je vends – I sell
le vendeur – seller
un garçon – boy
une fille – girl

Refer also to vocabulary for different fruits and phrases for buying goods in Units 4, 5 and 7.

Extension:

Quel parfum ? – What flavour?
abricot (m) – apricot
ananas (m) – pineapple
cerise (f) – cherry
citron (m) – lemon
menthe (f) – mint
pistache (f) – pistachio
poire (f) – pear
praline (f) – praline
un café – cafe
une/deux boule(s) – one/two scoop(s)
le marchand/le vendeur de glaces – ice-cream seller

Key phrases

Core:

C'est délicieux – It's delicious
J'aime les glaces – I like ice cream
Tu aimes les glaces ? – Do you like ice cream?
Je voudrais – I would like
Je voudrais une glace à la vanille/au chocolat – I would like a vanilla/chocolate ice cream
Qu'est-ce que tu voudrais ? – What would you like?

Extension:

J'adore les glaces ! – I love ice cream!
Je n'aime pas les glaces – I don't like ice cream
Combien de boules ? – How many scoops?
C'est combien ? – How much is it?
C'est tout ? – Is that everything?
Mes glaces sont délicieuses – My ice creams are delicious
La salade de fruits – fruit salad

Language points

- *Combien* can mean 'how much' or 'how many'. *C'est combien ?* is used for price; *Combien de ... ?* means, 'how many?' (quantity). The children may well have come across the same structure in *Combien de frères/sœurs as-tu ?* (How many brothers and sisters do you have?)

- Negatives are formed by adding *ne* before the verb and *pas* afterwards: *Je ne sais pas*. Note that *n'* is used where the verb begins with a vowel. *Je n'aime pas*.

- Possessive adjectives agree with the gender of the noun (singular): *ma glace, mon café*. In the plural there is no difference between masculine and feminine (*mes glaces, mes cafés*).

- Note the use of *au* (for masculine) or *à la* (for feminine) before the flavour of ice cream (*Je voudrais une glace au chocolat/à la vanille*). To keep it simple teach the children to ask for *une glace vanille/chocolat* instead.

Unit 9: Je vais au café

Objectives

To know everyday French words and phrases for buying drinks and snacks in a café; to be able to express preferences about them.

Introducing the vocabulary

- Using 'Interactive flashcard: *Les boissons*', introduce the core vocabulary items starting with drinks.
- Ask the children which drink they would prefer, for example *Tu préfères un coca ou une limonade ?*
- Repeat the activity with snacks, using 'Interactive flashcard: *Les casse-croûtes 1*' and 'Interactive flashcard: *Les casse-croûtes 2*' depending on the ability of the class.
- Teach the children how to say *J'ai faim/J'ai soif* and to ask for a particular item, for example, *J'ai soif ; je voudrais une limonade*.

Vocabulary extension

- Use 'Interactive flashcard: *Les casse-croûtes 2*' to introduce the Extension vocabulary. Note that *des chips* is a 'false friend' (see Language points in Unit 5).

Core activities

- Discuss the differences between a café in France and in Britain. Many cafés have chairs and tables outside (on *la terrasse*): discuss reasons for this (climate, custom). Explain that French cafés sell alcoholic drinks as well as other beverages.
- Introduce the next activity, which is to role play being in a café. Pretend to be the waiter/waitress and ask the children what they would like using *vous désirez ?* The children can practise this with a partner.
- Remind them that in France euros are used. Introduce *centimes* in units of ten if appropriate, for example 2€ 50.
- Show 'Film: *Au café*' and ask the children to listen carefully to identify what was ordered, and any familiar phrases. Use this to remind the children of useful phrases they have learned in other units such as *c'est combien, c'est tout* and *je prends*. Introduce a new phrase: *l'addition s'il vous plaît*.
- Let the children role play ordering drinks (and snacks if this has been covered) in a café, perhaps using the euros from photocopiable page 37 (*Euros*) and, if possible, some menus (see Cross-curricular ideas, right). (Note: you may need to display written prompts of the core phrases for reference.) When they are confident, the children could act out their role plays for other classes.

Extension activities

- Distribute copies of photocopiable page 42 (*Recette de croque-monsieur*). The children will already be familiar with some of the vocabulary from other units; additional words and phrases have been provided above, in the Extension word lists, right.
- Go through the list of ingredients and ask the children to look at the quantities first. What do they think *tranche* means?
- Ask the children to try to work out the ingredients, giving prompts, such as: *What shape do you think the slices of ham are? What do you think fromage râpé might be?* Apply the rule of adding 's' after the circumflex. Do they know what a 'rasp' is in English? (A file; a grating noise.) Do they know what *crème fraîche* is? Is there an English word for it?
- Ask the children to read each instruction and try to draw a small appropriate illustration using coloured pencils on a separate sheet.
- You may want to point out that the verb forms are all commands (imperatives).

Resources

Interactive flashcards:
Les boissons
Les casse-croûtes 1
Les casse-croûtes 2

Interactive activity:
Au café

Photocopiable page 42:
Recette de croque-monsieur

Translation: *Recette de croque-monsieur*

Film: *Au café*

Film transcript: *Au café*

Preparation

Euro coins created from photocopiable page 37:
Euros

Interactive whiteboard

Unit 9: Je vais au café

Cross-curricular ideas

D&T: To learn how to make a *croque-monsieur*.

Provide the children with ingredients to make their own *croque-monsieur*.

ICT: To use ICT to create a cafe menu.

Challenge the children to design their own menu for a French café, using ICT and the vocabulary that they have just learned.

Five-minute follow-ups

- When taking the class register, the children can pretend that you are the waiter/ waitress and place an order with you, such as: *Je voudrais un coca s'il vous plaît.*
- Children can practise the new vocabulary using 'Interactive activity: *Au café*' where missing words need to be added to complete a phrase.

Tips

Unit 23 '*Monter un café*' (Creating a café) of the QCA KS2 French Scheme of Work contains many more ideas for developing this unit.

Key words

Core:

les boissons (m) – drinks

un jus d'orange – orange juice

une limonade – lemonade

un coca – a cola

de l'eau – some water

un café – black coffee

un café-crème – white coffee

un chocolat chaud – hot chocolat

un thé – tea

les casse-croûtes (m) – snacks

un sandwich au jambon – ham sandwich

un sandwich au fromage – cheese sandwich

un croque-monsieur – ham and cheese toasted sandwich

une crêpe – pancake

Extension:

la terrasse – terrace/ outdoor area of a café

des chips (m) – crisps

des frites (f) – chips

une pizza – pizza

un sandwich au pâté – a pâté sandwich

un sandwich au saucisson – a continental sausage sandwich

la recette – recipe

sans – without

Language points

- *J'ai faim* and *J'ai soif* literally mean 'I have hunger', 'I have thirst' but there is no need to explain this to the children at this stage.
- Like ice-cream flavours (see Unit 8) types of sandwich are preceded by *à l'*, *à la* and *au*.
- *Vous désirez ?* and *C'est tout ?* are statements turned into questions. Encourage the children to ask questions in a 'rising tone' to make the meaning clear.

Key phrases

Core:

Je voudrais – I would like

J'ai soif – I'm thirsty

J'ai faim – I'm hungry

Monsieur/mademoiselle/madame – Excuse me (to summon the attention of the waiter/waitress; literally sir/miss/madam)

Vous désirez ? – What would you like?

Je préfère – I prefer

Tu préfères ... ou ... ? – Do you prefer... or...?

L'addition s'il vous plaît – The bill please

Extension:

une tranche carrée de pain/fromage – a square slice of bread/cheese

du fromage râpé – grated cheese

une tranche carrée de jambon – a square slice of ham

une cuillère à soupe de ... – a soup spoon of...

lave les mains ! – wash your hands!

étale la/le ... sur ... – spread the... on...

pose ... sur – arrange... on...

mets ... sur ... – put... on...

avec un peu de beurre – with a little butter

le four chaud – a hot oven

sors du four – take out of the oven

attends quelques minutes – wait a few minutes

avant de manger – before eating

température du four – oven temperature

See also vocabulary for different fruits and phrases for buying goods from Units 4, 5 and 7.

 Bon appétit ! Everyday French

Unit 10: Le déjeuner à l'école

Objective

To learn the names of foods from French school menus and to make comparisons with their own school menu.

Introducing the vocabulary

- Quickly revise the days of the week (including *samedi* and *dimanche* for completeness).
- Tell the children that together you are going to look at weekly menus from a French school. You are not going to tell them what the words mean but you will help them to say the words. Explain that they will recognise some of the words from the work they did on vegetables and fruits (Units 4 and 5).
- Give each child a copy of photocopiable page 43 (*Menu scolaire*).
- Go through some of the daily menus and ask the children to look for clues about the meaning of the words. Do some of the words look like words in English? (These are called cognates or *mots transparents* in French.) Can they make sensible guesses? Encourage the children to take risks in their guesses and not to be afraid of making mistakes. If all else fails, only then reach for the dictionary!

Core activities

- Pick one day's menu that you haven't looked at together and ask the children to try writing a translation on paper or mini whiteboards.
- Distribute your school menu for the following week. Ask the children to compare it with the French menu and talk about differences and similarities.
- Tell the children that you are going to try to work out (translate) what the school menu will be for just one day next week in French. Take a vote on which day they think will be easiest to do. Ask them which one will be the most difficult. Explain that French and English people don't always eat the same things so some dishes are untranslatable. If appropriate explain that you sometimes see some very odd English translations of menus in France. It isn't easy even for adults!
- Work through the day's menu on the whiteboard or ask the children to use bilingual dictionaries individually or in groups. Make copies of the day's menu in French for children in other classes to see.
- Using the plastic items or Interactive flashcards invite the children to talk about their preferences, for example:
Tu aimes/préfères les bananes ou les poires ? – Je préfère les bananes.
Vous aimez les choux de Bruxelles ? – Non, je déteste les choux de Bruxelles/Oui, j'adore les choux de Bruxelles.

Extension activities

- Distribute photocopiable page 43 (*Menu scolaire*). Ask the children to look at the menu for the second week and to pick out their preference by the day, for example: *Je préfère mardi/Je n'aime pas vendredi*. Try to elicit a reason by using *pourquoi ?* (for example: *Je déteste le poisson. Pourquoi ? C'est horrible !*).
- Introduce *Berk, je n'aime pas ça !* and *Miam miam, c'est délicieux !* Ask questions to elicit strong responses, for example: *Tu aimes le poisson ? – Berk, je n'aime pas ça, c'est horrible !*
- Ask the children to work in pairs and to put some drama and gesture into their dialogue so that they can act them out in front of the rest of the class.

Resources

Interactive flashcards:
Des légumes
Des fruits

Interactive activity:
Le déjeuner à l'école

Photocopiable page 43:
Menu scolaire

Preparation

Only the top half of the photocopiable is required for the core activities; the bottom half can be omitted initially if preferred.

Copies of your school menu for the following week

Plastic or real vegetables as props

French dictionaries

Interactive whiteboard

Unit 10: Le déjeuner à l'école

Tips

You will find a video and photographs of a French teacher demonstrating how to make little books at **www.pour-enfants.fr/video/petit-livre.htm**

Cross-curricular ideas

ICT/D&T: To design a weekly or daily menu or a packed-lunch diary.

Make little folding books of the week's menus (*Les menus de la semaine*) in French to place on the lunch tables. Children who have a packed lunch can do a diary for the week of the contents of their lunch box: *Mon panier-repas*.

PSHE/IU: Explain that French children do not generally go to school on Wednesday afternoons but sometimes meals are provided. Children don't usually take a packed lunch but many go home for lunch.

Five-minute follow-ups

- There is plenty of scope in this unit for work on the continuum: *j'adore ...*, *j'aime ...*, *je préfère ...*, *je n'aime pas ...*, *je déteste ...* perhaps using vocabulary from Unit 4 (*Au marché*) and Unit 5 (*Salade de fruits*).
- Play Chinese whispers with some of the new words and phrases.
- Play guessing games by mouthing the words only.
- Using 'Interactive activity: *Le déjeuner à l'école*', ask the children to create sentences by arranging the words in the correct order. Alternatively, the children can complete 'Interactive activity: *Le déjeuner à l'école*'.

Key words

Core:

la semaine – the week
lundi – Monday
mardi – Tuesday
mercredi – Wednesday
jeudi – Thursday
vendredi – Friday
samedi – Saturday
dimanche – Sunday
le menu – menu
la cantine – dining hall/canteen
le panier-repas – lunch box
(*l'*)*entrée* – starter
(*le*) *plat* – main course
(*la*) *viande* – meat
(*le*) *légume* – vegetable
(*le*) *fromage* – cheese
(*le*) *dessert* – dessert
les choux de Bruxelles – Brussels sprouts

Extension:

et – and
mais – but
pourquoi – why
parce que – because

Key phrases

Core:

J'adore – I love
Tu préfères – You prefer
J'aime – I like
Je n'aime pas – I don't like
Tu préfères ... ? – Do you prefer...? (to one child)
Vous préférez ... ? – Do you prefer...? (to whole class)
Je déteste – I hate
C'est délicieux – It's delicious
C'est horrible – it's horrible

Extension:

Berk, je n'aime pas ça ! – Yuk, I hate that!
Miam miam, c'est délicieux ! – Yum yum, it's delicious!
Bon appétit tout le monde ! – Enjoy your meal everyone!
Je suis végétarien (m) – I am a vegetarian
Je suis végétarienne (f) – I am a vegetarian

Language points

- Unlike in English, the days of the week in French are written in lower case.
- To make a verb negative *ne* is put in front of the verb and *pas* after it. *Ne* becomes *n'* in front of a vowel or an 'h'.
- The article *le, la, l', les* and *du, de la, des* is usually omitted when words form a list, as in the menus.
- When expressing likes and dislikes of foods it is usual to use *le, la, les*, for example *j'aime les bananes* and *je n'aime pas les carottes* as these are distinct categories of food.

Unit 11: Les spécialités françaises

Objectives

To locate regions in French using a map and compass directions; to learn about French food and drink specialities and some regional dishes.

Introducing the vocabulary

- Using copies of photocopiable page 44 (*La carte des régions*), introduce the geographical terms from the list of core words. First of all establish that children understand the four compass points in English, then give the French equivalents. Point to the five different regions shown on the map and read out their names, asking the children to listen and repeat (*Écoutez et répétez*).

- Ask questions such as: *Où est la Provence ?* to elicit the response *La Provence est dans le sud de la France.*

- Ask the children if they know of any foods and drinks that are special to France. Make a list of their suggestions. These may include cheese, wine and bread. The children may also suggest frogs' legs and snails. This is a useful opportunity to dispel some misconceptions about French eating habits (see Cross-curricular ideas).

Core activities

- French wines are famous throughout the world. Ask the children if they have heard of any. French cheeses are also world famous. There are around 400 cheeses made in France. Ask the children if they know any (be prepared for some 'wrong' answers from other countries). It is said that there is one cheese for every day of the year and there are some common sayings or proverbs about cheese. Here are some to display on the whiteboard:

- *Il n'y a pas de bon repas sans fromage* – There's no (such thing as a) good meal without cheese.

- *Une journée sans fromage est comme une journée sans soleil* – A day without cheese is like a day without sunshine.

- Explain that *sans* means 'without' and ask the children if they can work out what the sayings mean. Invite the children to practise saying one of the sayings as if they were advertising cheese on television.

- Use *Une journée sans fromage est comme une journée sans soleil* as an advertisement writing frame for the children to substitute different foods of their choice. Encourage the children to use vocabulary they have learned in previous units, for example *Une journée sans fruits est comme une journée sans soleil*.

Extension activities

- Show the children a map of France (see 'Tips', right) and explain that France is roughly twice the surface area of the UK with a similar population of around 60 million.

- The country is divided into *départements* which are broadly equivalent to counties and the *départements* are grouped into *régions*. There are 22 *régions* including the island of Corsica (*la Corse*), which the children may not realise is part of France.

- Using the map from the photocopiable page 44, show the children the five highlighted *régions* and say that each has particular specialities (as do all the other regions of France). These include:

  > *La Bretagne : les crêpes, le cidre, le poisson*
  > *La Normandie : le lait, le beurre, le fromage, les pommes*
  > *La Bourgogne : le vin*
  > *L'Aquitaine : le vin*
  > *La Provence : les fruits, les légumes, les fruits de mer*

- Explain to the children that the types of regional foods available influence the dishes that are produced and that climate and local conditions also have a bearing.

Unit 11: Les spécialités françaises

Cross-curricular ideas

PSHE/IU: To learn about cultural differences between countries and peoples.
Dispel any stereotypical ideas about French cuisine by explaining that both frogs' legs and snails are a delicacy and are eaten only rarely. The English term 'frogs' legs' is a little misleading as only the thighs are eaten (*les cuisses de grenouille*). And although many people associate eating snails with France, they are in fact eaten as a delicacy in several countries in continental Europe.

ICT: To use a search engine to find ingredients for recipes.
Challenge the children to use a search engine to find ingredients for one of the following traditional recipes: *le bœuf bourgignon, la bouillabaisse, le cassoulet.*

Five-minute follow-ups

- Have a cheese-tasting session and ask the children to express their preferences (see Unit 10 for vocabulary).
- Using a map of the UK, talk about the geographical locations of towns and cities in French. You could also research regional specialities in the UK and compare these with the French specialities.
- Use 'Interactive activity: *Où habites-tu ?*' to reinforce children's understanding of compass points in French.

Tips

There is an excellent interactive map of France at **www.ngfl-cymru.org.uk/vtc/interactive_maps/france/france_map.html** which shows departments, regions, rivers, towns and topography.

Key words

Core:

la France – France
la région – the region
la carte – the map
le nord – the north
le sud – the south
l'est (m) – the east
l'ouest (m) – the west
la Provence – Provence
la Bourgogne – Burgundy
la Normandie – Normandy
la Bretagne – Brittany
l'Aquitaine – Aquitaine
la spécialité – speciality
un escargot – a snail
une grenouille – a frog
le vin – wine
le fromage – cheese
le pain – bread
sans – without
une journée – a day

Extension:

Note: Some of the terms below have no English translation so a description has been given.
le cassoulet – stew with beans and sausages
le bœuf bourgignon – beef stew made with wine
la bouillabaisse – stew made with fish and sea food
la ratatouille – stew made with tomatoes, aubergines and other vegetables
une crêpe – a thin pancake
un département – French administrative division, similar to a county in the UK
la Corse – Corsica

Key phrases

Core:

Où est ... ? – Where is...?
Dans le nord (de la France) – In the north (of France)
Dans le sud (de la France) – In the south (of France)
Dans l'est (de la France) – In the east (of France)
Dans l'ouest (de la France) – In the west (of France)

Extension:

un produit régional – a regional product
(*les produits régionaux* – regional products)
un plat régional – a regional dish
les fruits de mer – shellfish

Language points

- It is not expected that the children will learn the words for French regions other than the ones that have English equivalents. (Aquitaine is included because it was English territory from 1152 to 1453.)
- *Régional* (adjective) will change its spelling according to what is being described, for example *un produit régional* (m), *une spécialité régionale* (f) though this need not be emphasised.

Unit 12: Tout le monde parle français

Objective

To introduce some French-speaking countries and foods that they produce.

Introducing the vocabulary

- Explain to the children that French is not just spoken in France, but in many other places around the world. Tell them that they are going to find out about some of these places and about the food that is grown and produced there.
- Using real tropical fruits or 'Interactive flashcard: *Les fruits tropicaux*' introduce the words one by one, asking the children to listen and repeat (*Écoutez et répétez*).
- Now open 'Interactive map: *Des pays francophones*' and point to the map without activating the hotspot buttons. Say the names of the countries shown and ask the children to repeat them. Do the names have anything in common? (They all begin with *la.*) Can the children spot any other similarities?

Core activities

- Ask the children if they can think of any reasons why many countries around the world speak French. If they do not know, explain that they are former colonies – countries that were once ruled by France. Explain that five of these countries (*la Corse, la Réunion, la Guyane, la Guadeloupe* and *la Martinique*) have the status of French regions and the people who live there are French by nationality.
- Using the 'Interactive map: *Des pays francophones*', click on each of the French-speaking countries in turn beginning with Corsica (*la Corse*). The children will hear: the name of the country; whether it is an island and, if so, which sea or ocean it lies in; information about the climate and about the main crops and goods, for example:

    > *La Corse, c'est une île dans la mer Méditerranée.*
    > *Ici on parle français.*
    > *Il fait chaud ici.*
    > *On cultive les marrons et les olives.*
    > *On produit du fromage et du vin aussi.*

    (Note: the French region la Martinique has not been labelled due to the size and scale of the interactive map.)
- Listen to the scripts again, encouraging the children to make educated guesses about the meaning of words, for eaxmple *une île.* Explain that *marron* is the word for brown (not maroon!). Ask: *What crop might it be*?
- Go through the other countries in the same way asking the children to repeat the words for the seas/oceans, countries, products and crops. Vary the questioning and repetition.
- Explain that many of the countries are tropical islands (*une île tropicale*). Ask: *Which is the odd one out?* (*La Corse*) *Which country is not an island?* (*La Guyane*)

Extension activities

- Explain to the children that '*Tout le monde parle français*' has two meanings: it can mean 'the whole world speaks French' or 'everybody speaks French'. The children may be surprised to find out that they already use some French words in their everyday English language, especially words to do with foods. Can they explain why this might be? (The Norman Conquest, the dominance of French cuisine in the 19th century and so on.)
- Give the children photocopiable page 45 (*Mots cachés*) and ask them to find the French food words. They may not know what all the words mean so go through some of the more difficult ones together. Ask them to look up some of the words in a French/English dictionary. Are the meanings exactly the same (for example *cuisine*)?
- Explain that both English and French, like all languages, are evolving constantly and that some English food words are now common in French, for example: *un hot dog, un hamburger, un snack, un sandwich, un nugget*. Can the children give reasons as to why this might be? (The influence of the American fast food market.)

Resources

Interactive flashcard: *Les fruits tropicaux*

Interactive activity: *Ici on parle français*

Interactive map: *Des pays francophones*

Photocopiable page 45: *Mots cachés*

Preparation

English/French dictionaries

A world map (optional)

Interactive whiteboard

Unit 12: Tout le monde parle Français

Cross-curricular ideas

Geography: To explore a contrasting overseas locality.
La francophonie provides an ideal opportunity to link French with geography and explore a contrasting overseas locality. Visit **www.qca.org.uk/qca_5224.aspx** for a downloadable unit plan focusing on *La Réunion*.

Five-minute follow-ups

- Tell the children there are many more francophone countries which have influenced French cooking and restaurants in France. These include: *l'Algérie* (Algeria), *le Maroc* (Morocco), *le Vietnam* (Vietnam), *la Tunisie* (Tunisia). Can they find these countries on a world map? Which continent are they in? Which is the odd one out? In which continent is it? (Vietnam, in Asia (*l'Asie*))
- Play 'Interactive: *Ici on parle français*' – as a whole-class or individual activity. Double click on the flags to hear the names of the countries spoken.

Key words

Core:

la Réunion – Reunion Island

la Corse – Corsica

la Guyane (française) – (French) Guyana

la Guadeloupe – Guadeloupe

la Martinique – Martinique

la Nouvelle-Calédonie – New Caledonia

les noix de coco (f) – coconuts

les papayes (f) – papayas

les bananes (f) – bananas

les goyaves (f) – guavas

les litchis (m) – lychee

les ananas (m) – pineapples

les figues (f) – figs

les mangues (f) – mangoes

les kiwis (m) – kiwis

les fruits de la passion (f) – passion fruit

les marrons (m) – chestnuts

les olives (f) – olives

l'huile d'olive (f) – olive oil

le sucre (à canne) – (cane) sugar

la vanille – vanilla

le riz – rice

le maïs – sweetcorn

les aubergines (f) – aubergines

un Français – a French man or person

une Française – a French woman

une région – a region

la francophonie – countries where French is spoken

tout le monde – everybody/the whole world

Language points

- *Un Français* is a French man; *une Française* is a French woman. *Le français* (lower case) is the language and adjective.
- Countries and continents that end in '*ie*' in French, often end in 'ia' in English, for example *l'Asie, l'Algérie*.
- *On* literally means 'one' but has come to mean 'we'. *On* also avoids the use of the passive in French. The children need not be given the full explanation.

Key phrases

Core:

(C'est) une île tropicale – (It's) a tropical island

les fruits tropicaux – tropical fruits

Ici on parle français – Here we speak French/Here French is spoken

Ici on cultive ... – Here we grow.../ Here...is grown

Ici on produit ... – Here we produce.../ Here...is produced

Il fait (très) chaud – It's (very) hot

Ce n'est pas une île tropicale – It isn't a tropical island

la mer Méditerranée – the Mediterranean Sea

l'Océan Atlantique – the Atlantic Ocean

l'Océan Pacifique – the Pacific Ocean

l'Océan Indien – the Indian Ocean

l'Amérique du Sud – South America

Extension:

Tout le monde parle français – Everyone speaks French/The whole world speaks French

Quelle heure est-il ?

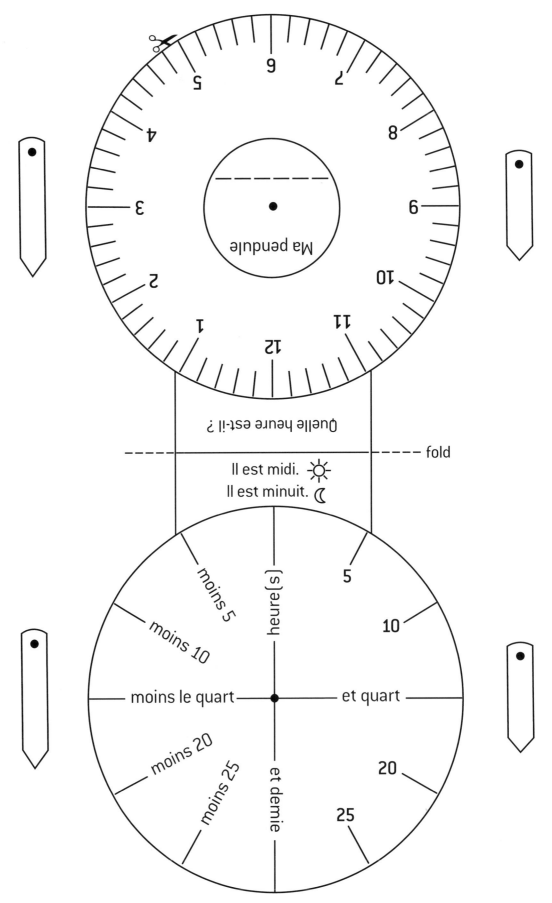

Ma pendule

Quelle heure est-il ?

- fold

Il est midi. ☀
Il est minuit. ☾

moins 5
moins 10
moins le quart
moins 20
moins 25
heure(s)
et demie
5
10
et quart
20
25

Photocopiable

Un set de table

Illustration © Joanna Kerr / New Division Ltd

Everyday French Bon appétit !

SCHOLASTIC
www.scholastic.co.uk Photocopiable

Le petit déjeuner

une baguette	de la confiture
du chocolat chaud	du café
du jus d'orange	une brioche
un croissant	un verre
un bol de chocolat chaud/de café	du beurre

Euros

Avec mon panier

Avec mon panier, je vais au marché.
Qu'est-ce que tu as donc dans ton panier ?
Moi, j'ai une pomme.
Moi, j'ai une pomme.

Avec mon panier, je vais au marché.
Qu'est-ce que tu as donc dans ton panier ?
Moi, j'ai une pêche.
Moi, j'ai une pomme.

Avec mon panier, je vais au marché.
Qu'est-ce que tu as donc dans ton panier ?
Moi, j'ai une poire.
Moi, j'ai une pêche.
Moi, j'ai une pomme.

Avec mon panier, je vais au marché.
Qu'est-ce que tu as donc dans ton panier ?
Moi, j'ai une fraise.
Moi, j'ai une poire.
Moi, j'ai une pêche.
Moi, j'ai une pomme.

Avec mon panier, je vais au marché.
Qu'est-ce que tu as donc dans ton panier ?
Un kilo de pommes.
Un kilo de pommes.

Avec mon panier, je vais au marché.
Qu'est-ce que tu as donc dans ton panier ?
Un kilo de pêches.
Un kilo de pommes.

Avec mon panier, je vais au marché.
Qu'est-ce que tu as donc dans ton panier ?
Un kilo de poires.
Un kilo de pêches.
Un kilo de pommes.

Avec mon panier, je vais au marché.
Qu'est-ce que tu as donc dans ton panier ?
Un kilo de fraises.
Un kilo de poires.
Un kilo de pêches.
Un kilo de pommes.

Un petit bonhomme

C'est un petit bonhomme
petit, petit, petit

Sa tête est une pomme

Son nez est un raisin
Son corps est une orange

Ses deux bras sont des poires
Sa jambe est une banane

Son autre jambe aussi

C'est un petit bonhomme
petit, petit, petit

C'est un petit bonhomme
tout fait avec des fruits

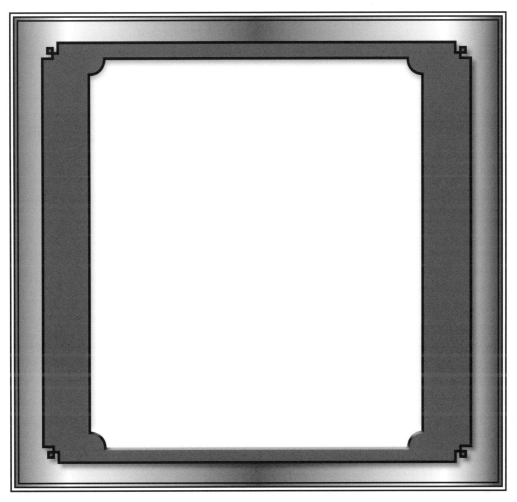

SCHOLASTIC
www.scholastic.co.uk Photocopiable

Everyday French Bon appétit ! 39

Allons aux magasins !

la charcuterie	la fromagerie
la pâtisserie	la boucherie
la boulangerie	le marché
l'épicerie	l'hypermarché
la poissonnerie	le supermarché
la crémerie	la confiserie

Le vendeur de glaces

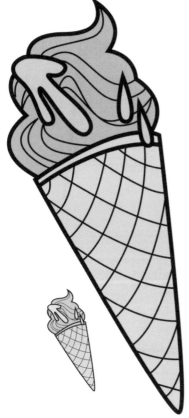

Moi, je vends des glaces
Dans le grand marché
Abricot, banane,
Chocolat, café.
Ah bonjour, ma fille.
Qu'est-ce que tu voudrais ?
Je voudrais une vanille,
Monsieur, s'il vous plaît.

Moi, je vends des glaces
Dans le grand marché
Abricot, banane,
Chocolat, café.
Ah bonjour, Martine,
Qu'est-ce que tu voudrais ?
Je voudrais une praline,
Monsieur, s'il vous plaît.

Moi, je vends des glaces
Dans le grand marché
Abricot, banane,
Chocolat, café.
Ah bonjour, Suzanne.
Qu'est-ce que tu voudrais ?
Je voudrais une banane,
Monsieur, s'il vous plaît.

Moi, je vends des glaces
Dans le grand marché
Abricot, banane,
Chocolat, café.
Ah bonjour, mon garçon.
Qu'est-ce que tu voudrais ?
Je voudrais un citron,
Monsieur, s'il vous plaît.

Illustration © Joanna Kerr / New Division Ltd

Recette de croque-monsieur

(Pour 2 personnes)

Ingrédients :
4 tranches de pain
2 tranches de fromage (Gruyère, Emmenthal)
30 grammes de fromage râpé
2 tranches carrées de jambon
10 grammes de beurre
2 cuillères à soupe de crème fraîche

Température du four : 200°

Méthode :

1. Lave les mains !
2. Étale la crème fraîche sur deux tranches de pain.
3. Pose une tranche de jambon sur les deux tranches de pain.
4. Pose une tranche de fromage sur le jambon.
5. Pose une tranche de pain (sans crème fraîche) sur le fromage.
6. Mets du fromage râpé sur les croque-monsieur préparés, avec un peu de beurre.
7. Mets les croque-monsieur dans le four chaud pendant 10 minutes.
8. Sors les croque-monsieur du four.

Attention !
Les croque-monsieur sont très chauds ! Attends quelques minutes avant de manger.

Bon appétit !

Menu scolaire

Menu de la semaine du 9 au 13 juin

	lundi	mardi	mercredi	jeudi	vendredi
Entrée	Salade de tomates	Salade de riz	Melon	Radis/beurre	Pizza
Viande	Bœuf	Rôti de jambon	Steak haché	Filet de poulet	Poisson à la crème
Légume	Carottes	Petits pois	Pommes de terre vapeur	Courgettes et pommes de terre	Haricots verts
Fromage	Fromage	Fromage	Fromage	Yaourt arôme nature	Camembert
Dessert	Crêpes au chocolat	Fraises crème chantilly	Nectarine	Compote de pommes	Fruits frais

Menu de la semaine du 16 au 20 juin

	lundi	mardi	mercredi	jeudi	vendredi
Entrée	Salade verte	Carottes râpées	Pâté au porc	Œuf dur mayonnaise	Betteraves vinaigrette
Viande	Poulet	Couscous à l'agneau et ses légumes	Omelette aux fines herbes	Poisson sauce tomate et oignons	Escalope de dinde aux pruneaux
Légume	Gratin de pommes de terre	—	Chou-fleur sauce tomate	Lentilles et carottes	Pâtes et ratatouille
Fromage	Emmental	—	Port Salut	Yaourt aux fruits mixtes	Fromage régional
Dessert	Pâtisserie: éclair parfum café	Flan	Nectarine	Biscuit aux amandes	Fruit de saison

La carte des régions

Illustration © The Drawing Room

Mots cachés

e	b	e	u	g	n	i	r	e	m	j	c	a	f	é
h	w	o	k	a	e	ç	m	s	o	r	b	e	t	l
c	a	n	a	p	é	c	d	u	u	e	u	t	z	r
i	y	k	r	n	r	x	k	p	s	f	f	t	i	z
u	w	é	i	e	u	g	i	l	s	l	f	e	k	e
q	c	h	a	m	p	a	g	n	e	a	e	l	x	t
t	h	i	l	c	p	d	â	ç	û	m	t	e	v	t
n	e	f	c	u	û	é	t	u	a	s	û	m	h	e
e	f	s	é	i	y	a	e	û	v	e	b	o	n	r
n	q	w	j	z	r	é	a	t	e	m	r	u	o	g
i	b	o	d	b	a	g	u	e	t	t	e	s	t	i
s	o	u	f	f	l	é	e	m	d	p	é	g	û	a
i	v	c	r	u	d	i	t	é	s	û	t	b	o	n
u	r	e	s	t	a	u	r	a	n	t	â	i	r	i
c	r	o	i	s	s	a	n	t	f	i	p	o	c	v

café   omelette   quiche   canapé

restaurant   gâteau   baguette   vinaigrette

chef   croissant   sauté   crudités

champagne   cuisine   sorbet   croûton

buffet   mousse   soufflé   gourmet

éclair   pâté

meringue   purée

Illustration © Moreno Chiacchiera / Beehive Illustration

Glossary

General vocabulary

Common courtesies

Bonjour madame/monsieur
.... Hello madam/sir
Au revoir madame/monsieur
.... Goodbye madam/sir
Bon appétit ...... Enjoy your meal
S'il te/vous plaît .. Please
Voilà .... There you are
Merci .... Thank you

Expressing facts, opinions and preferences

C'est ... . It's...
bon .... good
coloré .... colourful
délicieux .... delicious
drôle .... funny
horrible .... horrible
original .... original
Il y a ... . There is/are
J'adore ... . I love...
J'aime ... . I like...
Je préfère ... . I prefer...
Je n'aime pas ... .. I don't like...
Je déteste ... . I hate...
Je mange ... . I eat, I am eating
Je prends ... . I (will) have/ take
Je voudrais ... . I would like...
Berk, je n'aime pas ça !
.... Yuk, I don't like that!
et .... and
mais .... but
pourquoi .... why
parce que .... because

Games/songs

Qu'est-ce qui manque ?
.... What's missing?
Jacques a dit ..... Simon says
Touchez la tête ... Touch your head
Je vais aux magasins pour acheter ...
.... I am going to the
                shops to buy...
Qu'est-ce que tu as donc dans ton panier ?
.... What do you have
                in your basket?
garçon (m) ...... boy
fille (f) .... girl
mots cachés ..... wordsearch

Useful questions

Qu'est-ce que c'est ?
.... What is it?
Qu'est-ce que tu préfères ... ou ... ?
.... Which do you prefer...
                or...?
Qu'est-ce que tu manges pour le petit déjeuner ?
.... What do you eat
                for breakfast?
Qu'est-ce que tu voudrais ?
.... What would you like?
Combien de (boules) ?
.... How many (scoops)?

Tu aimes (les glaces) ?
.... Do you like
                (ice cream)?
C'est tout ? .... Is that everything?
Avez-vous ... ? .... Do you have...?
C'est combien ? .. How much is that?
Quel parfum ? .... What flavour?

Topic-related vocabulary

Days of the week

lundi .... Monday
mardi .... Tuesday
mercredi .... Wednesday
jeudi .... Thursday
vendredi .... Friday
samedi .... Saturday
dimanche .... Sunday

Drinks

boisson (m) ...... drink
café (m) .... black coffee
café crème (m)... white coffee
chocolat chaud (m) hot chocolate
coca (m) .... cola
eau (f) .... water
jus d'orange (m).. orange juice
lait (m) .... milk
limonade (f) ..... lemonade
thé (m) .... tea
vin (m) .... wine

Eating healthily

C'est bon/mauvais pour la santé
.... It's healthy/unhealthy
Je mange bien, je mange sain
.... I eat well, I eat
                healthily
les produits sucrés et salés
.... sugary and salty foods
au moins cinq par jour
.... at least five a day

Eating out

Monsieur/mademoiselle/madame
.... Excuse me,
                (to summon the
                attention of the waiter/
                waitress; literally sir/
                miss/madam)
entrée (f) .... starter
plat (m) .... main course
dessert (m) ...... dessert
specialité (f) .... speciality
menu (m) .... menu
terrasse (f) ..... terrace/outdoor area
                of a cafe
Vous désirez ? .... What would you like?
Je voudrais... .... I would like...
J'ai soif .... I'm thirsty
J'ai faim. .... I'm hungry
L'addition s'il vous plaît
.... The bill please
repas (m) .... meal

le petit déjeuner .. breakfast
le déjeuner .... lunch

Eating at home

le goûter .... afternoon snack
                for children
le dîner .... dinner
C'est l'heure de manger
.... It's time to eat
Le petit déjeuner est à sept heures
.... Breakfast is at
                7 o'clock
Je prends/Je mange le déjeuner à midi
.... I have/eat lunch
                at midday
A table ! .... Time to eat!/
                Come to the table!

Food

abricot (m)...... apricot
ananas (m) ..... pineapple
aubergine (f) .... aubergine
baguette (f) ..... baguette/French loaf
banane (f) ...... banana
beurre (m) ...... butter
biscuit (m) ...... biscuit
bœuf bourguignon (m)
.... beef stew made
                with wine
bonbons (m pl) ... sweets
bouillabaisse (f) .. stew made with
                fish and seafood
brioche (f)....... brioche
carotte (f) ...... carrot
cassoulet (m) .... stew with beans and
                sausages
céréale (f) ...... cereal
cerise (m) ...... cherry
champignon (m) . mushroom
chips (m pl) ..... crisps
chocolat (m) .... chocolate
chou (m)........ cabbage
chou-fleur (m).... cauliflower
citron (m) ...... lemon
confiture (f)...... jam
couscous (m) .... couscous
crêpe (f) .... crêpe (pancake)
croissant (m) .... croissant
croque-monsieur (m)
.... ham and cheese
                toastie
cuisses de grenouilles (f pl)
.... frogs' legs
escargots (m pl).. snails
fines herbes (f pl). herbs
figue (f) .... fig
fraise (m) ...... strawberry
framboise (f) .... raspberry
frites (f pl) ...... chips
fromage (m) .... cheese
fruits (m pl) ..... fruit
fruit de la passion (f)
.... passion fruit
glace (f) .... ice cream
goyave (f)....... guava

haricots (verts) (m pl)
. . . . (green) beans
kiwi (m) . . . . kiwi
lard (m) . . . . bacon
légumes (m pl) . . . vegetables
litchi (m) . . . . lychee
maïs (m) . . . . sweetcorn
mangue (f) . . . . mango
marrons (m pl) . . . chestnuts
melon (m) . . . . melon
menthe (f) . . . . mint
noix de coco (f) . . . coconut
nourriture (f) . . . . . food
œuf (m) . . . . egg
oignon (m) . . . . onion
olives (f pl) . . . . . . olives
orange (f) . . . . orange
pain (m) . . . . bread
papaye (f) . . . . papaya
pâté (m) . . . . pâté
pâtes (f pl) . . . . . . pasta
pêche (f) . . . . peach
petits pois (m pl) . . peas
pizza (f) . . . . pizza
poire (f) . . . . pear
poisson (m) . . . . . fish
poivre (m) . . . . pepper
poivron rouge/vert/jaune (m)
. . . . red/green/yellow
pepper
pomme (f) . . . . apple
pomme de terre (f) potato
prune (f) . . . . plum
quiche (f) . . . . quiche
raisin (m) . . . . grape
raisins secs (m pl) raisins
ratatouille (f) . . . . stew made with
tomatoes, aubergines
and other vegetables
riz (m) . . . . rice
salade de fruits (f) fruit salad
sandwich (au jambon/au fromage) (m)
. . . . (ham/cheese)
sandwich
sauce (vinaigrette) (f)
. . . . (vinaigrette) sauce
saucisses (f pl) . . . sausages
saucisson (m) . . . . continental sausage
sel (m) . . . . salt
toast (m)/*pain grillé* (m)
. . . . toast
tomate (f) . . . . tomato
viande (f) . . . . meat
yaourt (m) . . . . yoghurt

Geography

Où est ... ? . . . . . Where is ...?
la France . . . . France
la région . . . . the region
la carte . . . . the map
le nord . . . . the north
le sud . . . . the south
l'est . . . . the east
l'ouest . . . . the west

l'Aquitaine . . . . Aquitaine
la Bourgogne . . . . . Burgundy
la Bretagne . . . . . . Brittany
la Normandie . . . . Normandy
la Provence . . . . . . Provence
la Corse . . . . Corsica
la Guadeloupe . . . . Guadeloupe
la Guyane (française)
. . . . (French) Guyana
la Nouvelle-Calédonie
. . . . New Caledonia
la Réunion . . . . . . Reunion Island

Household objects

assiette (f) . . . . plate
bol (m) . . . . bowl
couteau (m) . . . . . . knife
cuillère (f) . . . . spoon
fourchette (f) . . . . . fork
plateau (m) . . . . . . tray
table (f) . . . . table
tasse (f) . . . . cup
verre (m) . . . . glass

Numbers

un, deux, trois, quatre, cinq, six, sept, huit, neuf, dix . . . . numbers 1–10

Parts of the body

bouche (f) . . . . mouth
bras (m) . . . . arm
corps (m) . . . . body
jambe (f) . . . . leg
main (f) . . . . hand
nez (m) . . . . nose
oreilles (f pl) . . . . . ears
pied (m) . . . . foot
tête (f) . . . . head

Shopping

boucherie (f) . . . . . butcher
boulangerie (f) . . . bakery
café (m) . . . . café
charcuterie (f) . . . . cooked meat shop
confiserie (f) . . . . . sweet shop
crémerie (f) . . . . . . dairy shop
épicerie (f) . . . . . . grocery
fromagerie (f) . . . . cheese shop
hypermarché (m) . hypermarket/
superstore
magasin (m) . . . . . shop
marché (m) . . . . . . market
pâtisserie (f) . . . . . cake shop
poissonnerie (f) . . fishmonger
supermarché (m) . supermarket
client/cliente (m/f) customer
vendeur/vendeuse (m/f)
. . . . stallholder
Je vais au marché. I go/am going to the
market
Je vais aux magasins pour acheter ...
. . . . I am going to the shops
to buy...
un kilo de ... . 1kg of...
un demi-kilo de ... . 1/2kg of...

deux cents grammes de ...
. . . . 200g of...
... et aussi ... .and also...
C'est tout ? . . . . . . Is that everything?
Avez-vous ... ? . . . . Do you have...?
Je vends ... . I sell...
Je regrette, je n'ai pas de ...
. . . . Sorry, I don't have
any...
C'est combien ? . . How much is that?
Ça coûte ... . It costs...
deux euros s'il vous plaît
. . . . 2 euros please
une/deux boule(s) one/two scoop(s)
un morceau (de fromage)
. . . . a piece (of cheese)
un pot (de yaourt) a pot (of yoghurt)
une boîte (de thon) . . . . . . a tin (of tuna)
une bouteille (d'eau minérale)
. . . . a bottle
(of mineral water)
une tranche (de jambon)
. . . . a slice (of ham)

Telling the time

Quelle heure est-il ?
. . . . What time is it?
Il est ... . It's...
... une heure . . . . . . 1 o'clock
... deux heures . . . . 2 o'clock
... trois heures . . . . 3 o'clock
... quatre heures . . 4 o'clock
... cinq heures . . . . 5 o'clock
... six heures . . . . . . 6 o'clock
... sept heures . . . . 7 o'clock
... huit heures . . . . . 8 o'clock
... neuf heures . . . . 9 o'clock
... dix heures . . . . . . 10 o'clock
... onze heures . . . . 11 o'clock
... midi . . . . midday
... minuit . . . . midnight
Il est sept heures cinq
. . . . It's five past seven
Il est sept heures dix
. . . . It's ten past seven
Il est sept heures et quart
. . . . It's quarter past seven
Il est sept heures vingt
. . . . It's 20 past seven
Il est sept heures vingt-cinq
. . . . It's 25 past seven
Il est sept heures et demie
. . . . It's half past seven
Il est huit heures moins vingt-cinq
. . . . It's 25 to eight
Il est huit heures moins vingt
. . . . It's 20 to eight
Il est huit heures moins le quart
. . . . It's quarter to eight
Il est huit heures moins dix
. . . . It's ten to eight
Il est huit heures moins cinq
. . . . It's five to eight

Contents

Counting to 3

Count and colour the toys.

Draw 2 ears on each animal.

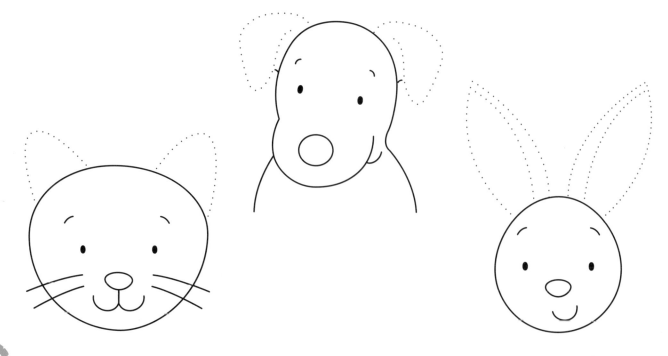

4

Counting to 5

Draw 5 kites.

The twins are 5 today. Draw the candles on each birthday cake.

Zero

Count the marbles in each jar.

 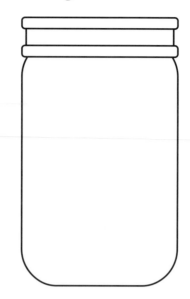 

Draw lines to match the vases with zero flowers to the number 0.

0

Recognising numbers to 5

Help the girl jump across all the stepping stones to get to the other side. Say each number.

Colour the right number of toys in each row.

Counting to 8

Count and colour each kind of food.

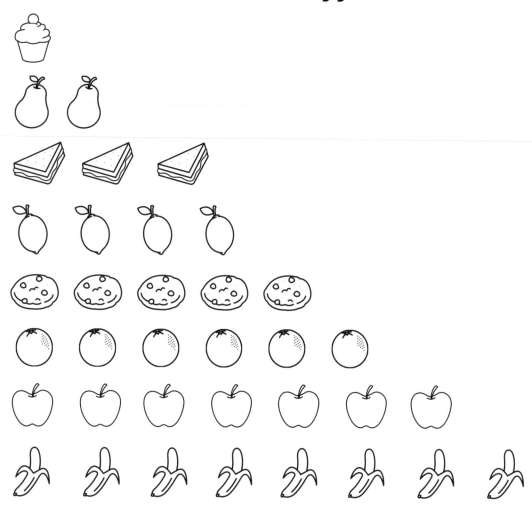

Draw 8 fish in the sea.

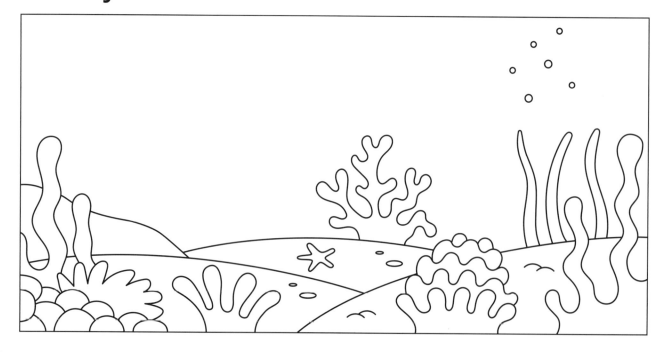

Counting to 10

Count and draw a ring around the 10 butterflies.

Colour the dog that has 10 spots.

Recognising numbers 6 to 10

Colour the right number of clothes on each washing line.

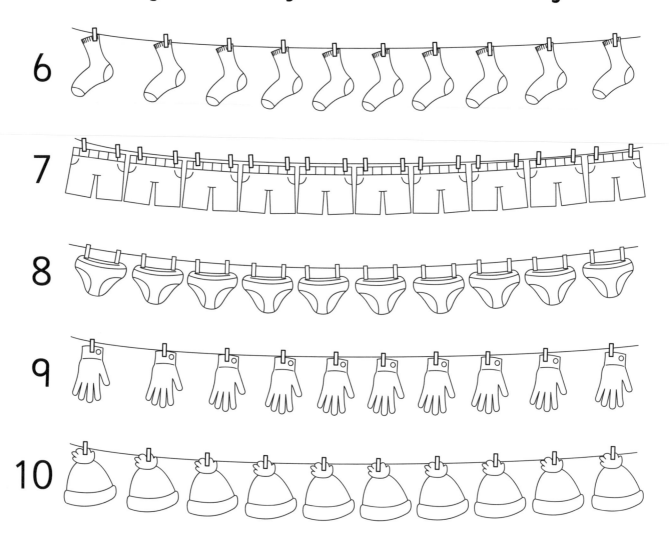

Draw a ring around the odd one out in each group.

Recognising numbers to 10

Count the animals in each field. Draw lines to match each picture to the right number.

1 2 3 4 5 6 7 8 9 10

Join the dots of the toy pictures.

Numbers around us

Draw lines to help each letter get to the right house.

Draw a ring around each of the numbers in the picture.

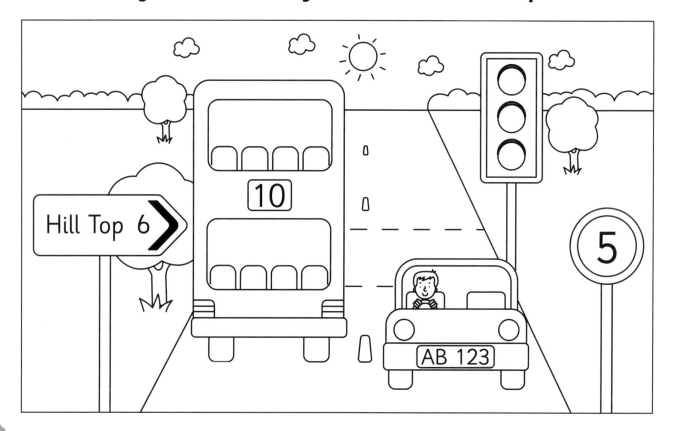

How many?

Count the sweets and draw a ring around the right number.

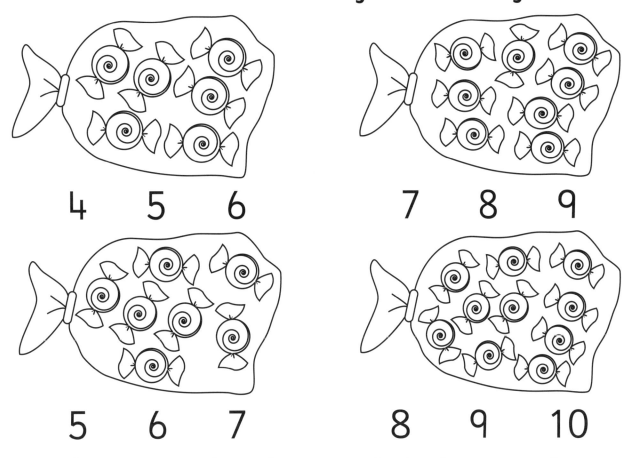

4   5   6   7   8   9

5   6   7   8   9   10

Draw lines to match each group of mini-beasts to the right number.

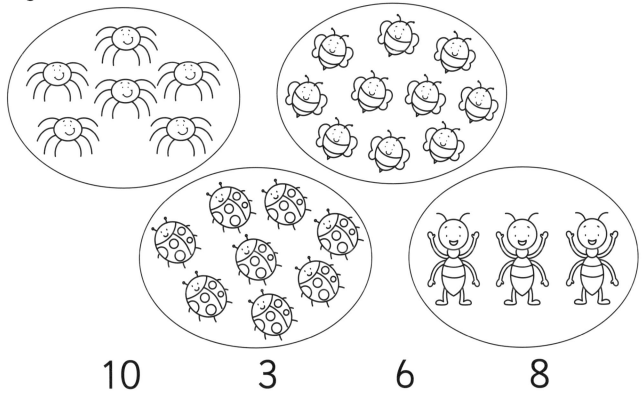

10   3   6   8

Sequencing to 5

Draw the dice in the right order up to 5.

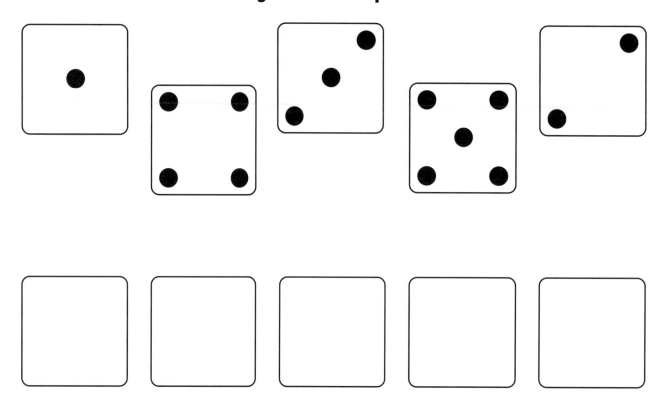

Follow the numbers in the right order to help the dog find her dinner.

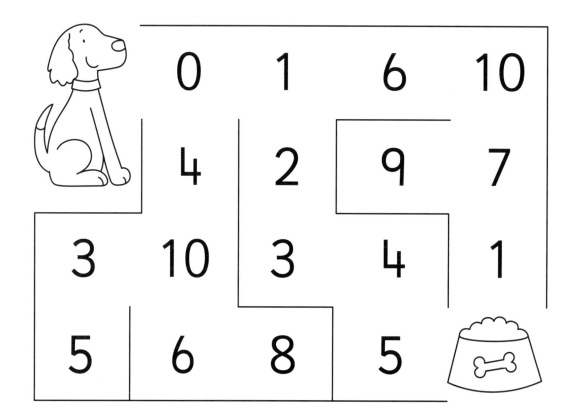

Sequencing to 10

Look at the daisy chain. Say the missing numbers.

Draw what comes next in each sequence.

Counting

Sequencing back from 5

Colour the rocket. Then say the countdown to lift-off!

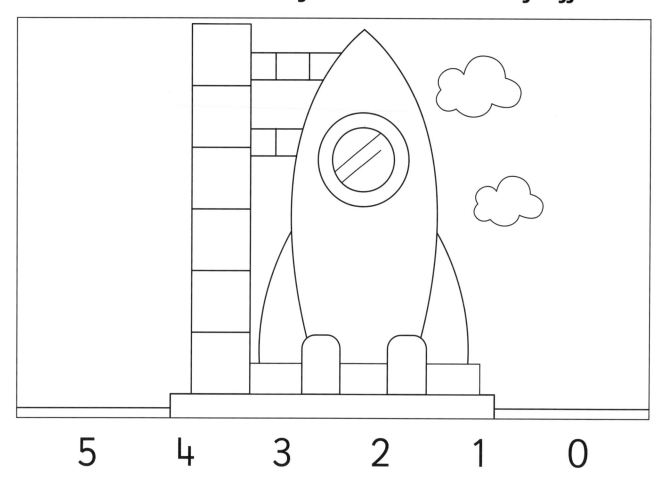

5   4   3   2   1   0

Draw lines to join the dragon's eggs in order from 5 to 1.

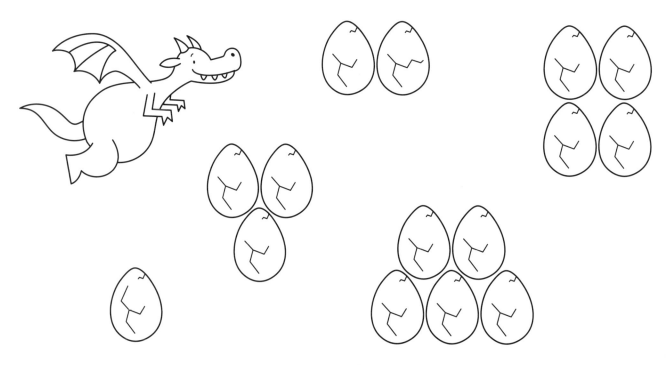

16

Sequencing back from 10

Draw what comes next in each sequence.

Count backwards to join the dots of the elephant picture.

Writing numbers 0, 1 and 2

Count the animals. Then trace and copy the number.

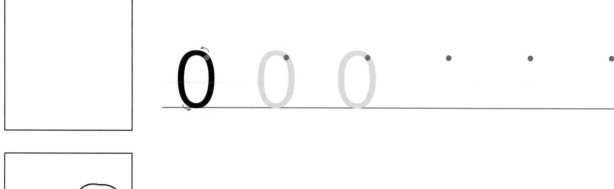

Count and write how many of each vegetable there are.

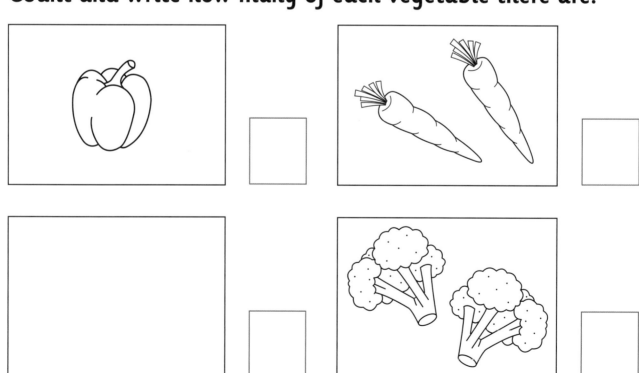

Writing numbers 3, 4 and 5

Count the cakes. Then trace and copy the number.

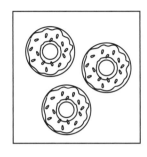

3 3 3

4 4 4

5 5 5

Count and write how many treats each child has made.

Writing numbers 6, 7 and 8

Count the animals. Then trace and copy the number.

6 6 6

7 7 7

8 8 8

Count and write how many teeth each monster has.

Writing numbers 9 and 10

Count the objects. Then trace and copy the number.

9 9 9 • • •

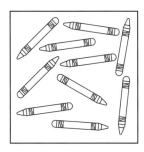

10 10 • • • • •

Count and write how many balls there are.

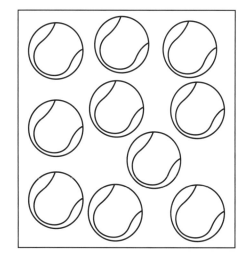

Counting to 15

Help the shopkeeper count the things on each shelf in
his shop.

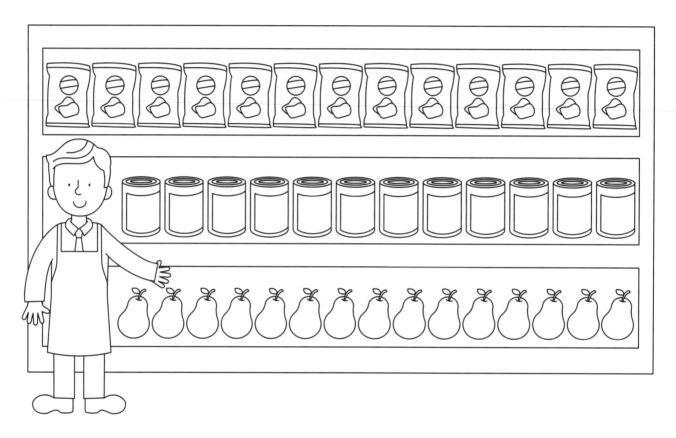

Count and colour the 15 shells.

Counting to 20

Draw more bows on the kite string to make 20 altogether.

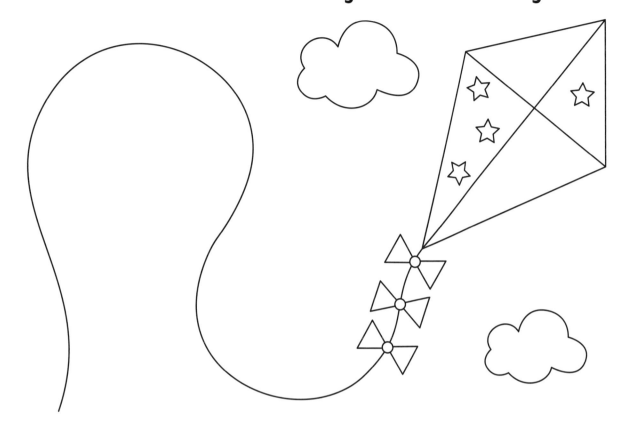

Draw a monster with 20 arms.

Recognising numbers to 15

Draw a ring around all the numbers.

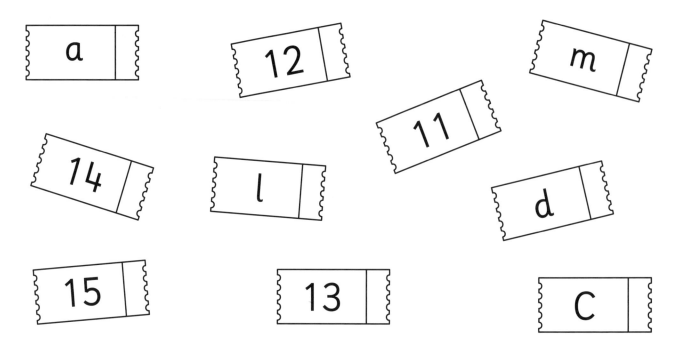

Colour the fish by numbers.

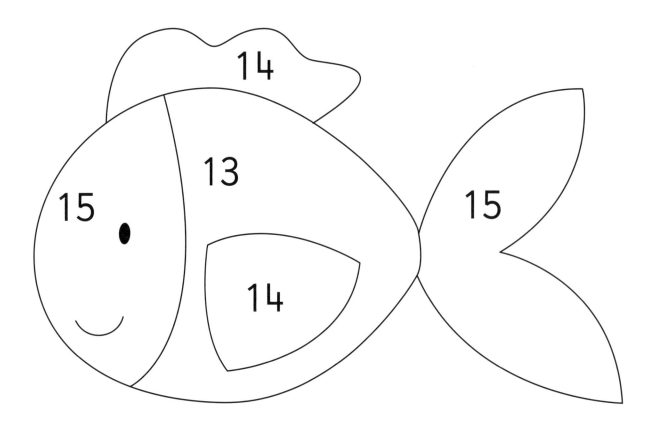

13 red   14 purple   15 yellow

Recognising numbers to 20

Draw lines to match each group of objects to the right number.

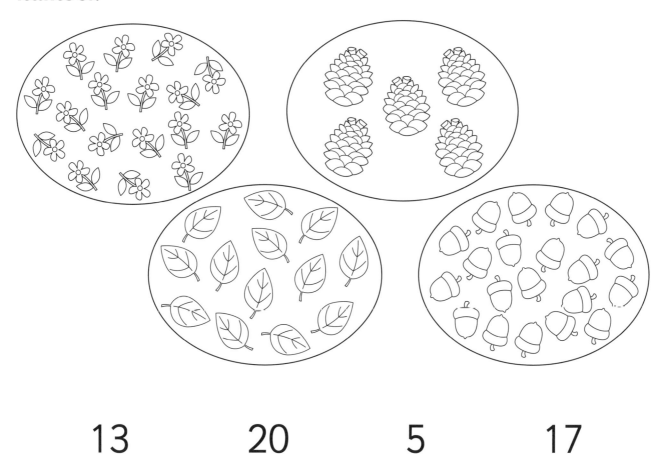

13   20   5   17

Join the dots of the snail picture.

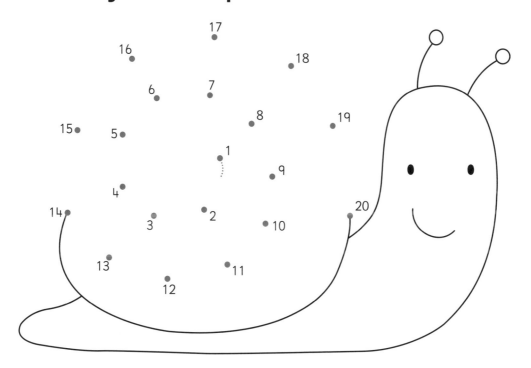

Writing numbers to 15

Write the numbers on the sails.

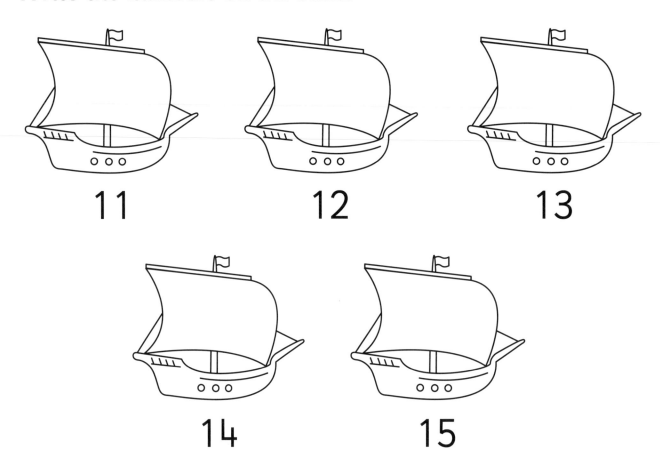

11   12   13

14   15

Count and write how many animals there are.

Writing numbers to 20

Write the numbers on the football shirts.

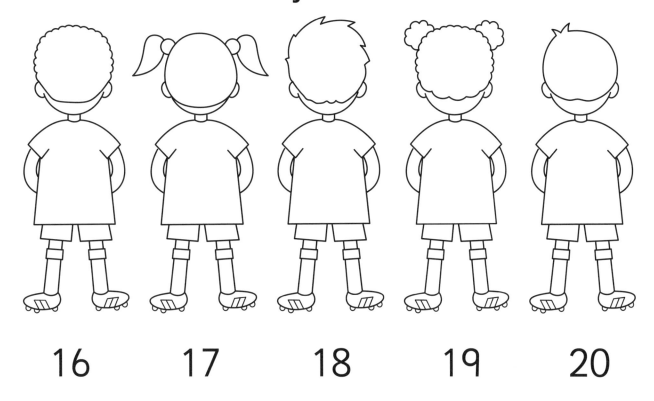

16   17   18   19   20

Count and write how many spots there are on the butterflies.

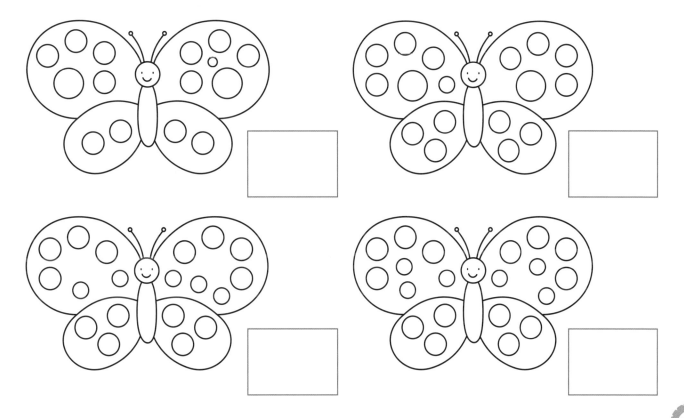

Sequencing to 20

Follow the numbers in the right order to help the pirate find the treasure.

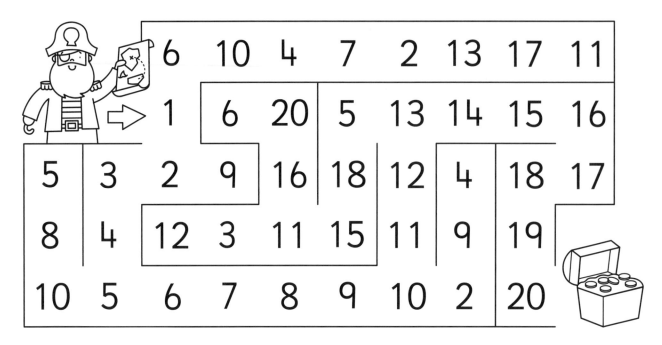

Write the missing numbers on the train carriages.

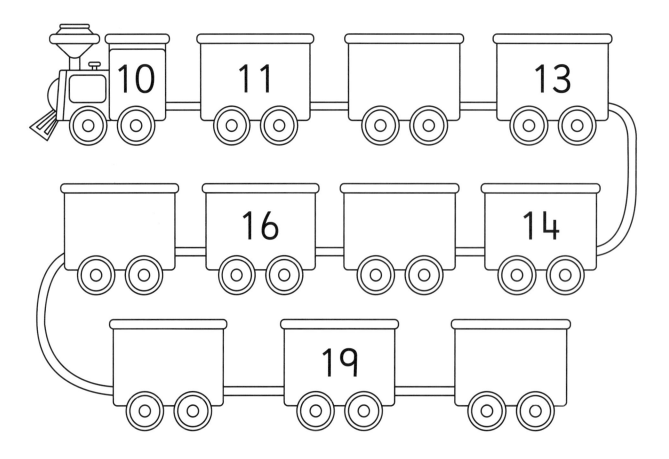

Sequencing back from 20

Count backwards and draw lines to help the frog cross the pond.

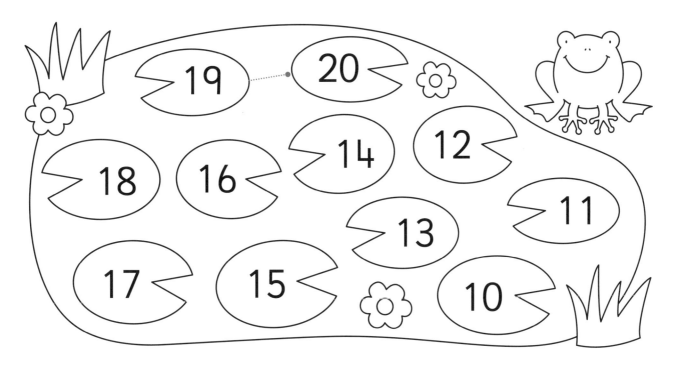

Count backwards and write the missing numbers on the glow worms.

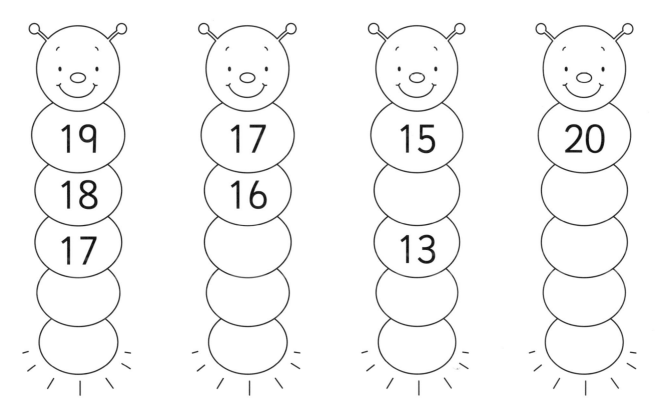

Notes for parents and carers

Topic	Teaching tip	Key vocabulary	Extension activity
Counting to 3 page 4	Encourage your child to point at each object and count aloud.	number, count, one, two, three	Ask your child to count and collect toys or objects from around your home into groups of 3.
Counting to 5 page 5	Spend time talking about how or why we know how many candles there should be on each cake.	count on, count up to, three, four, five	Talk about birthdays with your child and ask them what else might have numbers on (for example, cards, balloons, badges).
Zero page 6	Explain that the empty vases have 'zero flowers' in them, as it can be hard for children to understand that 'zero' means 'nothing'.	number, zero, nothing, none, empty	Throw counters into a hoop or pot, one after another. Have 5 counters each and count how many you get in the target. Use the word 'zero' if it was none.
Recognising numbers to 5 page 7	To continue the activity, ask your child to count how many toys are not coloured in each row.	one, two, three, four, five	Place some large numbers 0 to 5 on the floor. Play Musical bumps with your child. Each time the music stops, you call a number and they find it and sit on it.
Counting to 8 page 8	Using toy food, help your child to collect and count food items to match the pictures.	six, seven, eight, many, few	Go outside and make a collection of 8 objects (for example, leaves, pebbles, shells, twigs or anything else your child is interested in). Count them together.
Counting to 10 page 9	Show your child how to make tally marks to help them count the butterflies and dots.	nine, ten, too many, too few, altogether	Sing a counting rhyme together, such as 'One, two, three, four, five – once I caught a fish alive'.
Recognising numbers 6 to 10 page 10	Use a number track (a long strip of squares with a number in each one) to help your child to identify each number.	row, group, recognise, same, different	Think of an action together for each number from 6 to 10, and draw it next to the number. Show the numbers out of order and ask your child to name the number and do the action.
Recognising numbers to 10 page 11	Encourage your child to say the numbers aloud when they are completing the dot-to-dot pictures.	number, check, order, group, how many?	Make the numbers 1 to 10 with play dough and ask your child to read them aloud. They collect each number as they read it and make a big play-dough ball.
Numbers around us page 12	Talk about why the envelopes have numbers on them. Ask your child how the numbers help, and what number your house is.	address, house number, road sign, number plate, different	Go for a number hunt around the house. Ask your child what numbers they recognise on the clock, calendar, washing machine or TV.
How many? page 13	Encourage your child to guess how many sweets or mini-beasts there are first, and then to count the objects to find the total.	group, how many?, guess, more, fewer	Help your child to make their own animal out of junk-modelling materials, including a number of legs, wings or antennae to count.
Sequencing to 5 page 14	Provide your child with a number track, so they can check that they have sequenced the numbers correctly.	sequence, forwards, order, follow, carry on	Make some cookies together and number them with icing. When eaten as treats over the next few days, they must be eaten in order.
Sequencing to 10 page 15	Help your child to count out loud, in sequence, to find the missing numbers.	sequence, missing, before, after, what comes next?	Make some stepping stones out of card and number them from 0 to 10. Ask your child to place them in order, to get across the shark-infested water!
Sequencing back from 5 page 16	Encourage your child to use an animated voice when counting down to lift-off.	count back, direction, countdown, up, down	Say the rhyme 'Zoom, zoom, zoom, We're going to the moon – 5, 4, 3, 2, 1, Lift-off!' together as you play space rockets.

Get Set Mathematics

Topic	Teaching tip	Key vocabulary	Extension activity
Sequencing back from 10 page 17	Ask your child to talk about what they are doing when they are drawing.	sequence, backwards, what comes next?, carry on, count back	Help your child collect groups of toy cars or animals to sequence backwards (for example, 10 horses, 9 cows, 8 sheep).
Writing numbers 0, 1 and 2 page 18	Encourage your child to trace the numbers carefully with their finger first, and to begin at the correct starting point.	start, end, zero, one, two	Do some 'air writing' together. Draw a number as large as you can in the air and encourage your child to copy it. Then swap round.
Writing numbers 3, 4 and 5 page 19	Help your child form the numbers by moving in the correct direction.	top, bottom, three, four, five	Encourage your child to write numbers with their finger in sand, salt or flour.
Writing numbers 6, 7 and 8 page 20	Encourage your child to copy the numbers if they need to. Provide a number track or write out the numbers for them to refer to and copy.	curved, straight, six, seven, eight	Using sandpaper numbers (sand glued to number outlines), challenge your child to guess the number without looking.
Writing numbers 9 and 10 page 21	Make sure your child understands that they are writing the number 10 and not the separate numbers 1 and 0.	starting point, follow, trace, nine, ten	Trace numbers on your child's back and challenge them to recognise the number you have written.
Counting to 15 page 22	Encourage your child to say the numbers aloud. Listen for the correct pronunciation.	eleven, twelve, thirteen, fourteen, fifteen	Help your child to cut out and stick on to paper 15 of their favourite toys from a catalogue.
Counting to 20 page 23	Help your child to practise counting to 20 by counting when they go up or down stairs.	sixteen, seventeen, eighteen, nineteen, twenty	Ask your child to draw a picture of the night sky with 20 stars.
Recognising numbers to 15 page 24	Help your child to read the key before they start to colour the fish, as they may not yet be confident in reading the colour words.	eleven, twelve, thirteen, fourteen, fifteen	Make a 0-to-15 number fan (16 number cards held together with a split pin) with your child.
Recognising numbers to 20 page 25	Encourage your child to guess how many objects there are first, before counting them. Talk about whether the number that they guessed was too big or too small.	greater than, less than, count, count on, last	Create a number code for your child to crack (for example, if a=1, d=2 and m=3, 1213 spells 'Adam'). Make it spell out their name.
Writing numbers to 15 page 26	Make sure your child is comfortable when writing. Model how to hold a pencil correctly between the thumb and forefinger with the pencil resting on the third finger.	digit, straight, curved, practise, remember	Make the numbers 0 to 15 together using counters. Make sure your child begins placing the counters at the correct starting point when writing each number.
Writing numbers to 20 page 27	Encourage your child to say the numbers aloud when they are writing them.	shape, size, direction, height, movement	Talk with your child about large numbers of things (for example, cars on the road, stars in the sky, beans in a tin).
Sequencing to 20 page 28	Ask your child to count out loud, in sequence, to find the missing numbers.	start, end, finish, down, up	Have two plates, 20 small objects and tongs to use. Encourage your child to count to 20 while moving the objects from one plate to another.
Sequencing back from 20 page 29	Encourage your child to look for the largest number first when sequencing backwards.	starting point, top, across, direction, end	Play a game of Hide and seek, with the seeker slowly counting backwards from 20 each time.

Counting

Schofield & Sims

Help children to become school-ready with **Get Set Early Years**, an engaging cross-curricular programme to bridge the gap between play and formal learning.

Developed by experienced practitioners and based on the Early Years Foundation Stage framework, **Get Set Early Years** is designed to build confidence, encourage curiosity and foster a love of learning.

- exciting and motivating activities to support classroom teaching
- friendly illustrations that children can enjoy colouring in
- key vocabulary for each topic area, providing opportunities to create a rich language environment
- notes and tips for parents and carers to help you delve further into each topic

Get Set Mathematics: Counting develops children's early understanding of numbers, providing practice in counting, recognising and writing numbers, and sequencing. This book introduces young learners to numbers through a variety of activities, including count the objects, write the number, complete the picture and follow the sequence activities.

Discover the other **Get Set** activity books:

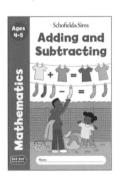

ISBN 978-07217-1436-3

9 780721 714363

MIX
Paper from responsible sources
FSC® C023114

ISBN 978 07217 1436 3
Early Years
Age range 4–5 years
£3.95 (Retail price)

For further information and to place your order visit
www.schofieldandsims.co.uk or telephone 01484 607080

Schofield&Sims

KS1 Problem Solving 3

45
small

31
medium

16
large

Name

KS1 Problem Solving
Book 3: Contents

by Anne Forster
and Paul Martin

KS1 Problem Solving

is a series of three books:

KS1 Problem Solving Book 1   978 07217 0922 2

KS1 Problem Solving Book 2   978 07217 0923 9

KS1 Problem Solving Book 3   978 07217 0924 6

Printed by Wyndeham Gait Ltd., Grimsby

© 2002 Schofield & Sims Ltd.

978 07217 0924 6

First Printed 2002
Twelfth impression 2012

Schofield & Sims Limited Huddersfield England